SYNCHRONIZED SWIMMING

Synchronized Swimming

FERN YATES

Assistant Professor of Physical Education
Barnard College, Columbia University

THERESA W. ANDERSON

Director of Physical Education for Girls
North High School, Des Moines, Iowa

Second Edition

THE RONALD PRESS COMPANY • NEW YORK

Library of Congress Catalog Card Number: 58-5645
PRINTED IN THE UNITED STATES OF AMERICA

FOREWORD

In these days when physical education tends to be associated in the popular mind primarily with winning teams and with the sports page, it is refreshing to find a book in which the emphasis is on rhythm, grace, precision and beauty. In the past, the physical education analogues of music and art have been confined largely to the dance forms, and to a lesser degree, in the minds of many, to beautifully skilled performances in the more individual or dual sports activities, such as diving, gymnastics, tennis and golf, where the more culturally-minded performers have sought to achieve the feeling of beauty as assiduously as they have sought excellence and accuracy of execution of the techniques.

Now, synchronized swimming has come into the picture. Here, to the other pleasures of swimming, has been added the pleasure inherent in water ballet and group coordination of effort—all performed to appropriate music and so executed as to compare favorably with the aesthetics of the dance. Synchronized swimming is a true cultural addition to the physical aspect of education.

Until the appearance of *Synchronized Swimming,* there has been no complete textbook for the guidance of those who wish to explore this new area. The present volume includes methods, techniques and formations, as well as many practical suggestions drawn from the rich experience of the authors.

The educational and teaching backgrounds of the two authors supplement each other almost ideally. Miss Fern Yates has had many years of experience teaching in a YWCA, in a Community House, and in a college environment, developing as one part of her program water shows and pageants, and experimenting with the creation of new art forms in this field. Mrs. Theresa Anderson has had an equally long experience in the field of secondary education, and, in the last few years, in addition to time spent on the creative side of synchronized swimming, has given much attention to the competitive aspect of this aesthetic activity. This combination of experiences and talents, together with the fine book making and the wealth of illustrations, makes this an outstandingly fine text and source book for those interested in this relatively new and intriguing field.

C. H. McCLOY, PH.D.
State University of Iowa

PREFACE

Synchronized Swimming explains how strokes and stunts may be taught to a rhythmic accompaniment, how synchronization in its simplest form may be employed as a teaching tool in swimming classes at any level of ability, and how synchronization may be developed into water compositions for programs, pageants, and competition. The material is progressively developed within each chapter, and from chapter to chapter, to make the book helpful to the inexperienced as well as to the experienced teacher and student. Methods are suggested for dramatizing programs through the use of staging effects. Over 300 underwater and surface photographs of swimmers in action illustrate the step-by-step procedures to follow in the execution of the strokes and stunts. Line drawings illustrate patterns a teacher can follow in class work and swimmers can use in designing water compositions.

The use of a rhythmic beat—that is, the timing of skills to music—is an effective teaching device and an organizational aid. The teacher who wants to introduce synchronization in regular swimming classes will find practical suggestions in this book for teaching skills to rhythm, in a progression, in a small area, and to several levels of ability. In the latter instance, for example, he learns how to organize his class in such a manner that, to a single piece of music, an elementary group practices the kick or the arm stroke, another group works on the entire stroke, and the more advanced group practices synchronizing with one another. In addition to employing synchronizing techniques as a teaching method and an organization aid, the book shows how synchronization offers an interesting way to demonstrate class work in a swimming exhibition.

Any experience a teacher gains in teaching synchronization in regular swimming classes is a great help in teaching special synchronized swimming classes. In these classes the swimmers know the strokes and probably the simple stunts, thus allowing the teacher to work on perfecting synchronization, gaining control of the body in the water, teaching additional stunts, and adapting water skills to express an idea or feeling of the music in a water composition. The book emphasizes the importance of independent practice of the four basic strokes to music and of individual synchronization of arm, leg, and body position to the group's position. Breath control, horizontal floating, and transitions from one stroke to another are discussed. The teach-

vii

ing hints offered throughout the chapters will aid those who teach swimming rhythmically, whether in regular or special synchronized swimming classes.

Combining the skills effectively involves appreciation of music and good composition. The book introduces the teacher to musical analyses and principles and acquaints a synchronized swimming class with structural form. To help the swimmer in the creation of water composition, ideas and practical suggestions for design and choreography are supplied.

For those interested in conducting a clinic, suggestions are included on the organization of a one-day session.

The material in the chapter on competition is adapted to various levels of synchronized swimming ability and includes suggestions on competition for simple stunt or water composition performances. Officials, teachers, and performers will find information on rules, multiple difficulty ratings for stunts, and a sample of a routine sheet and a judge's grading sheet.

The authors are deeply indebted to the following: Grover Hubbell, Arden McClain, and E. D. Weeks, together with the Des Moines Parks Department, for furnishing pool facilities to secure the illustrations; Howard Swift, Des Moines *Register* and *Tribune,* for assisting with the photography; JoAnn Speer Wormley, Des Moines (the only national champion in synchronized swimming to win championships in all three divisions—solo, duet, and team), for executing the stunts and strokes for the illustrations; Douglas Moore, Columbia University, whose book *Listening to Music* furnished some of the musical background; Olive McCormick, whose book *Water Pageants* furnished the idea of a pool mock wedding; and Rita Benson, Smith College, for contributing the campfire number in Chapter 8 and reading the manuscript.

Sincere appreciation is also extended to John A. Johnson and Lester D. Powell, Des Moines Public Schools, and C. H. McCloy, State University of Iowa, for their advice and cooperation; Margaret Holland and Marion Streng, Barnard College, and Betty Ebers, for reading the manuscript as well as making helpful suggestions; Jeanette E. Graustein, for assistance in editing the material; and to the authors' students, for their interest, efforts, and ideas, of which this book is a reflection.

FERN YATES
THERESA ANDERSON

CONTENTS

LIST OF STROKES AND STUNTS

LIST OF ILLUSTRATIONS

KEY TO THE FIGURES

— — — — —   Represents the path that the swimmer has already followed.

. . . .   Represents the path that the swimmer expects to follow.

$\big\uparrow = *1$ $\blacksquare\big| = *2$

SYNCHRONIZED
SWIMMING

1

NATURE OF SYNCHRONIZED SWIMMING

Swimming is said to be synchronized when two or more swimmers coordinate their movements to each other, or when one or more persons time swimming to a musical accompaniment. The emotional appeal of music makes the latter type of synchronization more pleasing to most people. Although synchronized swimming employs all the standard water skills, as the swimmers become proficient in their techniques and timing, they modify skills and arrange them to create a water composition which interprets the mood and framework of a musical selection or an idea.

It is not necessary to wait until students become proficient, nor to arrange special classes before introducing them to the technique of synchronizing. It can be started in classes at any level of ability, as soon as the swimmers achieve fair mastery of a skill. Even in classes whose major purposes is to teach only the standard skills, synchronizing skills can be a useful and enjoyable teaching device. It provides interest and fun for the class while the members practice the skill. It affords an incentive to the swimmer in that it illustrates a definite degree of accomplishment as the swimmer is able not only to perform the skill, but also to regulate his rhythm to that of the music or of another swimmer. It effectively demonstrates class work, contributes to rhythmic training, and provides an opportunity for teamwork in swimming.

Three elements indispensable to a synchronized swimmer are rhythm, a basic knowledge of the standard water skills, and creativeness. Rhythm is essential for all synchronized swimming. If music is not used, an underlying rhythmic beat can be felt by swimmers in a continual repetition of swimming skills or in a combination of them into a routine. The water skills are the standard strokes or stunts learned in swimming classes, which swimmers may combine into hybrid strokes or modify to make a water pattern or composition more effective. Once the swimmer has grasped the rhythmic idea and has learned the strokes, creative ability is of utmost importance, as he must then use his ingenuity to develop a water composition which is distinctive and artistic. Synchronized swimming is one field of aquatics that provides opportunity for, and encourages originality and expression of, ideas. These three

1

elements are taught progressively in all synchronized swimming classes. A water skill may be taught to a definite rhythm, then synchronized with music or with another swimmer. As experience grows, the swimmers learn to improvise and to develop their own patterns.

Further factors of great importance to the success of even the shortest routine are the ability to appreciate and analyze musical selections and an understanding of the principles of good composition. Students can develop these, too, with experience.

RHYTHM

A sense of rhythm is a quality which everyone possesses to some degree. From the very beginning both the instructor and the class find it helpful and interesting to use rhythm in the teaching and learning of water skills. Rhythm makes the learning process easier, quicker, and more enjoyable; it encourages the swimmer to relax; it teaches proper breathing habits; and it lays a good foundation for synchronized swimming.

Those who feel the rhythm can swing into it easily and begin to develop correct swimming habits. Many who are not conscious of the rhythm can learn with drill to recognize the underlying beat. The waltz, with its clearly defined phrases and accents, is the best rythm for general use, particularly at the beginning and intermediate levels and wherever new skills are being practiced.

It is not essential for the swimmers to hear music to develop a rhythmic response. The teacher may give his admonitions in ¾ time, he may clap the beat, or he may beat a drum, hit a woodblock or even a puck against a small kick board. Once the skill has been learned, use musical accompaniment in practice periods as, under its influence, swimmers concentrate on synchronizing their water skills with the music and relax their muscles unconsciously.

WATER SKILLS

The standard strokes and stunts are the main content of swimming classes, and proficiency in these basic skills is essential for synchronized swimming. Continual practice of a skill in the right way develops easy breathing and smooth, controlled movements. The student learns to use only those muscles essential to a particular effort, with no antagonistic ones working in conflict.

Introduce synchronization with music or with another swimmer as soon as the student demonstrates fair mastery of a skill. Swimming to rhythm helps the student learn the skills more easily and quickly, and, conversely, once the student learns the standard skills they provide the foundation for the modified and hybrid strokes used in advanced synchronized swimming. The many stunts in advance of the basic skills are a challenge to good swimmers, and the smooth performance of these stunts equips the swimmer with a wide range of skills for advanced work in synchronization.

CREATIVENESS

Like a sense of rhythm, the ability to create, to some degree, is universal. In many persons it needs recognition and encouragement; in others it needs guidance. Synchronized swimming is a field which presents many opportunities for those with the urge and capacity to create, both in the execution and in the conception of a water composition. The teacher soon discovers that some swimmers display great inventiveness and ingenuity in devising new water patterns, while others excel in translating those patterns into effective swimming compositions. Encourage both forms of creativity. Within the scope of synchronized swimming, those with originality and a strong rhythmic sense find great satisfaction in witnessing or participating in a performance of their own creation.

RECREATIONAL SWIMMING

In recent years, more persons have learned to swim than ever before. They have learned at an earlier age, and their leisure time has increased, giving them more opportunity for swimming. Most persons are not interested in competition but prefer to swim, play, and relax in the water for pure enjoyment. During a play period in swimming, children turn somersaults, stand on their hands, and roll over and over. They like the abandon which is possible in the water. When these children are shown the correct form of stunts with proper breathing, they are thrilled and eager to learn more. The same is true of older swimmers in perhaps a more conservative way. The performance of these skills in unison adds to their pleasure.

Synchronized swimming can be a source of great enjoyment to those who swim for fun. Swimmers like the discipline of synchronizing their strokes and stunts to the phrases of the music and with other swimmers. This stimulates an interest in the use of their skills and in learning new ones, and it also tends to prolong participation in the activity. Those who are experimental or who have had experience swim combinations of skills or improvise to the music, and interest others in doing the same.

SYNCHRONIZED SWIMMING CLASSES

Special classes in synchronized swimming are designed for the swimmers who are already proficient in the standard water techniques and who are therefore ready to modify strokes and stunts and to improvise in the water. These classes emphasize coordination of the skills of the group to attain perfect timing and unison of movement. These highly skilled classes offer the best opportunity for creative expression since they have the ability and the experience to produce longer and more intricate compositions, but even beginning and intermediate classes provide an outlet for the development of originality and imagination. Synchronization establishes for swimming a new area which utilizes watermanship, aqua-poise, rhythm, musical appreciation and imagination, thus offering the rich possibilities of a creative art.

2

MUSIC AND MUSICAL ACCOMPANIMENT

The emotional appeal of music is enjoyable and stimulating. Its use for swimming quickens the learning of skills and inspires and guides the development of water compositions.

Music of a simple rhythmic type with easily defined beats and phrases played at a tempo comfortable for swimming is excellent for teaching synchronization of skills to music in regular swimming classes and for practice in perfecting group synchronization in synchronized swimming classes. Familiar tunes, simply orchestrated, help the uninitiated synchronized swimmer to feel the rhythm and the phrasing quickly. The rhythms most commonly used are in 3/4 (waltz) and 2/4 or 4/4 time. An even, steady underlying beat in the music aids the swimmer in timing the swimming movements with the music.

The waltz, fox trot, march, pavane, tango, and so on are simply constructed rhythms that offer interesting variations in accent, tempo, expression, and appeal. The less exciting tunes are good accompaniment for the practice of techniques; all are suitable for introducing a group to water composition; and the orchestral arrangements of many of these dance rhythms, especially the music with interesting variations and contrasts, offer a challenge to the experienced synchronized swimmer for original expression.

There are many musical compositions of a more serious nature than dance tunes—short classical pieces, movements from suites and ballets—that offer inspiration and guidance for very interesting swimming designs. This type of music which may have changes in meter, in tempo, which may be impressionistic or very dynamic—calls for swimmers who are sensitive to the design and expression of the music and at the same time in command of a wide variety of skills, performed easily and smoothly. This combination of excellent skills and sensitivity to musical expression and movement enables the swimmer to harmonize effectively with the mood and rhythm of the music and achieve a water composition of a truly artistic nature.

4

MUSICAL TERMS AND MUSICAL ANALYSIS

Since music is such an important ally in swimming, both in teaching water skills and in creating compositions, it is well to understand basic terminology and certain fundamentals of construction. The expressive element of music is inexact and subjective while the structural design is exact. To achieve the best results with any type of music used for water composition it is necessary to understand the design of the musical piece—as a control and guide in designing the water composition.

DEFINITIONS. A *measure* is a unit of music that divides the fundamental rhythm at regular intervals; it usually has two, three, or four beats. A measure is commonly called a *bar*.

A *time signature* is a sign at the beginning of a composition or movement to indicate the rhythm or time in which the composition is to be played. It is always given in the form of a fraction—the denominator indicates the kind of note taken as a time unit for the beats; the numerator indicates the number of these beats to a measure. Time signatures commonly used for swimming are 2/4 (two-quarter measure), 3/4 (three-quarter measure), 4/4 (four-quarter measure), and 6/8 (six-eighths measure). A 2/4 measure indicates that there are two quarter-notes to each measure, or a total of two counts or beats, and so on.

The *accent* of a measure is that beat which is regularly stressed or emphasized. In 2/4 and 3/4 time, the first count in each measure is stressed and the others are weak; in 4/4 time the first count is strongest, the third not so strong, the second and fourth the weakest; in 6/8 the first is the strongest, the fourth not so strong, and the second, third, fifth, and sixth the weakest. The strongest count is called the *primary* accent; the next strongest, as the third one in 4/4 time, is the *secondary* accent. A syncopated effect may be achieved in any rhythm by accenting an off-beat.

A *phrase* in music is usually a grouping of four measures or bars at the end of which there is a natural break in the rhythm.

A *period* consists of two balanced phrases, usually eight measures; the first phrase has a suspensive ending, the second a more or less conclusive one.

Rhythm is the pattern the notes make, including the accents and rests, and is based on the regular occurrence of accents. Simple rhythm provides for one accent in a measure, as in 2/4 and 3/4 time; compound rhythm includes two accents, primary and secondary, as in 4/4 and 6/8 time.

Melody is a pleasing, rhythmical arrangement of a succession of single tones.

MUSICAL ANALYSIS. Play an American waltz record and tap out the accents and the weak beats. There is a regular count of *one,* two, three; *one,* two, three—each group of three indicating a measure of waltz music. Listen carefully and you will recognize at the end of every four measures a slight repose—the end of a phrase. The four measure phrasing occurs regularly, sometimes with a more or less suspensive ending and at another time with a feeling of finality. For each primary accent make a mark (/) on paper. Each mark indicates a measure. Group the marks into fours to indicate the phrases and link the phrases into periods.

After notating the measures and grouping them into phrases and periods, play the record over and over. It will help you to become aware of repetitions and variations of phrases, of contrasting phrases; it will help you to recognize a grouping of phrases into a short rhythmic pattern with accents and a sense of climax. The rhythmic pattern is commonly written in two or four phrases. The first such rhythmic pattern expresses a musical idea, a melodic theme, which is developed through repetition and variation of the theme, through the introduction of contrasting music that in some way relates to the theme, to the climax of the composition. The idea of the musical composition is then rounded out with a return to the first theme, either repeated or varied. The first theme and its development is called the *A Theme* and the *A Part,* the length of which varies considerably; the contrasting music which usually contains another theme is the *B Part* with the *B Theme;* and the return to the *A Theme* is the *A Part* again. There is usually an introduction of several measures, sometimes a few transitional measures to connect the contrasting parts, and often an ending or coda that may or may not recall both the *A* and *B* Themes. This *A B A* form or an expansion of it into *A B A B A* is the plan common to most of our good musical comedy airs, good dance music, short classical compositions, movements from ballets and suites. Composers may digress from the accepted pattern or follow a different one; knowing the usual form makes it easier to recognize others.

In developing a theme within a part, the composer often uses a short form of composition. One type of a short form, *A A B A,* is similar to that of the larger *A B A* form. As an example, in "Drink To Me Only With Thine Eyes" the *first A* represents a four measure phrase; the *second A* is a repetition of the phrase; *B* introduces a four measure phrase with a different melody and a change of accents; and the *last A* repeats the first phrase. There are variations in this short form, such as, *B* and each *A* may consist of eight measures instead of four; each repetition may have variations; or the last three phrases may be variations of the first, with the third one the most striking. Two other short forms are *A A A B* and *A A B B.* Wherever a different melodic phrase is introduced, the symbol changes.

Let us analyze a well-known piece of music, one that you can recall if you do not have the sheet music or the record: Beethoven's "Minuet In G," Victor 1434. Tapping the beats tells us it is written in 3/4 time, is slow in the first and last parts and fast in the middle. There are eighty measures or marks that divide into phrases of four measures and periods of eight //// ////. After thirty-two measures, the music changes for thirty-two measures, indicating the *B* part, and returns for sixteen measures to the first part, which makes the usual *A B A* form. There are no introductory, transitional, or coda measures. List these periods of eight measures one underneath the other with the letter after each. Bracket the first four periods as *A* of the large form, the next four as *B,* the last two as *A* again. Analyze each part: within the first *A* part the first period suggests the theme. //// //// —*A;* the second eight meassures repeat the *A* theme, //// //// —*A;* the third period is different,//// //// —*B;* the fourth repeats *B,* //// //// —*B,* so that within the large *A* part, there is a shorter form, *A A B B.* Within the large *B* part, the analysis is *C C D D.* In the second *A* part just one period of *A* and of *B* is recalled, *A B.* You can comment on the expression in the playing of the phrases and periods by making notations over or following them: for instance, put "Rit." (Ritardando) over the eighth phrase of the first part and over the fourth phrase of the last *A* part to indicate a slowing down of the tempo. Likewise, indicate loud or soft phrases, the fast *B* part, and the two slow *A* parts. With the form graphically noted and the comments about the expression of the music before you, you have an analytical picture of the music, a musical image, which guides the designing of the swimming movements.

Care has to be exercised in the selection of a piece of music for water composition in order to find an arrangement that is satisfactory without changing the musical structure. Omission of the repetition of a part may be musically acceptable but any deletions or change should be made by one versed in musical composition.

FORMS OF ACCOMPANIMENT

Recorded music is the most satisfactory method for accompanying synchronized swimming. The machine is convenient to use, produces varying degrees of volume, and keeps an even rhythm. A phonograph equipped with a speed regulator permits a larger selection of tunes for swimming because the tempo of the music may be adjusted to suit the requirements of the swimmers.

Choral singing is another satisfactory means for accompanying synchronized swimming. The singers must be sure to keep the rhythm and tempo even and definite and to sing the selection so that it is enjoyable yet not distracting for the swimmers as well as the audience. Choral singing as accompaniment has several advantages over recordings in that the musical arrangement of a piece can be adapted to the swimming situation and musical selections and parts of pieces that are not available on records may be sung. It also adds musical and dramatic interest to the water activities.

The same conditions apply to instrumental accompaniment as to choral singing. Almost any instrument may be used, provided the performers are competent.

SELECTION OF RECORDS

Consider the following comments when searching for suitable records for a machine without a speed regulator. The tempo of American waltzes varies from very slow to very fast; the tempo of Viennese waltzes in general is very fast. There are slow, quick, and double-quick marches. The slow marches—

the processional, recessional, triumphant, and funeral—are most likely to be satisfactory when played at a standard rate of speed. Fox trots offer great variety in tempo and mood. Consider carefully the music and the ability of the swimmers before making a selection.

To determine the desired tempo of a musical composition for swimming if the machine to be used does not have a speed regulator, first choose a waltz record that is satisfactory to the swimmers. With the second hand of a watch or stop watch, count the number of strokes per minute at the tempo the swimmers normally use. One crawl arm pull usually requires one measure of music. Second, count the number of measures, or arm pulls, per minute in the recording chosen to compare with the number the swimmers use. This comparison helps determine the advisability of buying the record. For instance, in the album *Popular American Waltzes,* played by Al Goodman, the records average forty bars to the minute, which means forty arm pulls; generally this is a good tempo for waltz rhythms. Remember that the mood and spirit of the music also influence its desirability as a swimming accompaniment. In the album *Continental Tangos,* played by Marek Weber, the records average thirty-two measures, or arm pulls, to the minute. This tempo, slower than that of the waltz, is satisfactory for tangos, but to swim slowly the swimmers must have a stronger crawl stroke. Russell Records of Ventura, California, issues a catalogue of records for dance, mainly ballet and tap, with the meter, number of bars, and playing time of each record listed. Some of these selections are suitable for synchronized swimming—for example, #42, "The Ballet Dancer" waltz, has about forty bars to a minute.

Listen to musical recordings over the radio with a critical ear. Since orchestras vary in their arrangements of the same tune, one or more of these arrangements may be suitable for your purposes. Instrumental recordings in general are preferable to those with a vocal chorus. In areas where record selections are limited, local radio stations may prove helpful in loaning records.

RECORD SUGGESTIONS

Irving Berlin, George Gershwin, Victor Herbert, Jerome Kern, Frederick Loewe, Cole Porter, Richard Rogers, Sigmund Romberg, and Vincent Youmans are composers of airs for musical comedies and musical drama that are suitable for swimming.

The following orchestra leaders play instrumental recordings of music by the above composers as well as by others: Les Baxter, Ray Bloch, Carmen Cavallerro, Frank Chackfield, Emile Coleman, Percy Faith, Robert Farnon, Arthur Fiedler, Al Goodman, Morton Gould, Andre Kostelanetz, Guy Lombardo, Vaughn Monroe, David Rose, Paul Weston, Claude Thornhill, Hugo Winterhalter, Marek Weber, Victor Young.

Below are examples of suites and ballets with one or more movements suitable for water compositions. However, not all orchestrations are suitable. Select thoughtfully from the various recordings as certain orchestrations would overpower the swimming—Benjamin Britten: *Peter Grimes Suite;* Delibes: *Sylvia Ballet;* Morton Gould: *Interplay;* Grieg: *Peer Gynt Suite;* Handel: *Water Music Suite;* Khachaturian: *Masquerade Suite;* Offenbach: "Can-Can" from *Gaité Parisienne;* Rodgers: "Slaughter On Tenth Avenue" from *On Your Toes;* Saint-Saens: "The Swan" from *Carnival of Animals;* Tchaikovsky: *Nutcracker Suite* and *Swan Lake.* The "March" from *Love for Three Oranges* by Prokofiev, the "Waltz" from *Eugin Onegin* by Tchaikovsky, the "Cornish Rhapsody" by Bath, and "Rhapsody In Blue" by Gershwin are suitable examples of opera selections and rhapsodies.

3

INTRODUCING SYNCHRONIZATION INTO REGULAR SWIMMING CLASSES

This chapter deals with synchronizing techniques, standard strokes, and basic stunts to 3/4 rhythm in the regular swimming classes. First the student learns and practices a skill across the pool, and an excellent method of instruction from the beginning is to teach the skills rhythmically. A definite rhythm can be conveyed through modulation of the voice and spacing of the admonitions. If music is available, the swimmers can practice the skills later to waltz time with emphasis on synchronizing the accent of the stroke with that of a measure. After the swimmers can synchronize the single skills fairly well across the pool to music, have them time them with other swimmers and then try combinations of skills.

To develop a sense of rhythm and confidence in teaching skills to rhythmic accompaniment, tap the underlying beat every time you hear music. Be sure that you recognize the accents of the measures and the phrasing of a waltz record before you introduce it to a class, and that you can tap the rhythm without the music. Practice on land the timing of the strokes to a waltz record. The radio and records of many dance tunes enable you to gain rhythmic practice easily, and the better developed your sense of rhythm is, the easier it is for you to keep the class on the rhythmic beat.

In places with limited pool facilities and crowded classes, you can introduce synchronization to great advantage: many skills can be synchronized back and forth across the pool and many swimming fundamentals practiced in a small area. Synchronizing reduces the tedium of practice. At the same time, it develops swimmers for specific synchronized swimming classes, or it may develop a potential nucleus of synchronized swimmers that will be the beginning of a synchronized swimming program in the school.

The short routines presented in this chapter may be used for practice or for simple demonstrations. No variations or modifications of the standard strokes and stunts are suggested here in line with the principle that basic water skills should be learned well first. The one exception is in the case of the front crawl stroke, in which the head is carried higher than in the standard stroke in order to watch other swimmers, and the legs are lower in the water to support the raised head.

TEACHING TO MUSIC

Forty-four measures or forty-four crawl arm pulls to a minute is a good waltz tempo for swimming at all levels of ability. This rate of movement encourages a relaxed and smooth stroke. Using this tempo for waltz records to teach the swimming strokes, it takes two measures to do one complete front or back crawl stroke with six kicks, one elementary backstroke with the glide, one side stroke with the glide, or one breast stroke with the glide. The accent of the stroke coincides with the accent of a measure of music. In the *crawl stroke,* each hand enters the water or each elbow lifts out of the water on the first beat of a measure, and each kick coincides with a beat of a measure—six crawl kicks to two 3/4 time measures, and two arm pulls. In the *elementary backstroke,* the arms and legs open during the first measure; the pull of the arms and the drive of the legs synchronize with the accent of the second measure. In the *side stroke,* the legs open and the arms move toward each other during the first measure; the legs drive together and the arms stretch to the gliding position on the accent of the second measure. In the *breast stroke,* the arms pull on the accent of the first measure; the legs open during the first measure and drive together on the accent of the second measure; the arms extend and glide during the second measure. Suitable records in 2/4 or 4/4 time are also good accompaniment for the elementary back, side, and breast strokes.

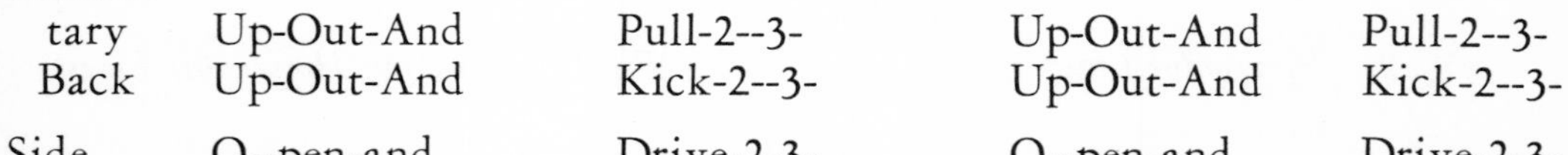

Crawl	Pull-2--3- Stroke----	Pull-2--3- Stroke----	Pull-2--3- Stroke----	Pull-2--3- Stroke----
Elemen- tary Back	Up-Out-And Up-Out-And	Pull-2--3- Kick-2--3-	Up-Out-And Up-Out-And	Pull-2--3- Kick-2--3-
Side	O--pen-and Pull-2--3-	Drive-2-3- Push-2--3-	O--pen-and Pull-2--3-	Drive-2-3- Push-2--3-
Breast	Pull-2--3-	Drive-2-3-	Pull-2--3-	Drive-2-3-

Fig. 1.   Four-measure Phrase

Each phrase of waltz music at this tempo synchronizes with two complete swimming strokes. Alternate admonitions for synchronizing the stroke with a four measure phrase of music are given in Figure 1.

5. Shallow standing dive
6. Plunge dive: hold breath and glide through the water with arms, legs, and body straight
7. Reverse turns for overarm stroke (Plate 2)
8. Foot first porpoise dive
9. Log roll
10. Back somersault
11. Front somersault
12. Handstand in chest deep water
13. Porpoise or surface dive-pike
14. Shark circle
15. Dolphin
16. Marching on water
17. Marlin turn
18. Standing dive

COMBINATION OF SKILLS. A combination consists of two or three of the above skills with the change from one to another usually taking place in the center of the pool. Since this change requires agility and skill, its accomplishment indicates definite advancement. Possible combinations follow. In Numbers 1 to 23, direct the swimmers, after changing skills in the center, to continue on across the pool; in Numbers 24 up to 30, instruct them to return to their starting places.

1. Push off and glide on face to center; roll onto back, pull arms to side, and take one elementary backstroke across.
2. Push off and glide on back with arms at side to center; roll onto face and crawl kick across with nose in water.
3. Push off on back, take two elementary backstrokes to center; roll onto face, dog paddle or elementary crawl across.
4. Push off on back, fin or back crawl kick to center; roll onto face, dog paddle or elementary crawl across.
5. Elementary crawl to center; roll onto back and elementary backstroke across.
6. Elementary crawl to center; roll onto back and back crawl kick and fin.
7. Sitting dive and glide to center; roll onto back and backstroke across.
8. Sitting dive and glide to center; roll onto back and fin with back crawl kick across.
9. Front crawl to center; roll onto back and back crawl across.
10. Front crawl to center; roll onto back and take one arm pull of the back crawl, roll onto face and front crawl across.
11. Back crawl to center; roll onto face and front crawl across.
12. Back crawl to center; roll onto face and take one arm pull of the front crawl, roll onto back and back crawl across.
13. Push off and side stroke to center; roll onto the other side and continue side stroke across.
14. Push off and side stroke to center; describe a six-foot circle with four side strokes with back to center of the circle and continue side stroke across (Fig. 5).

15. Push off and side stroke to center; shark circle stunt and side stroke across (Fig. 5).
16. Push off and side overarm stroke to center; roll onto the other side and continue side overarm across.
17. Push off and side overarm stroke to center; describe a six-foot circle with four side strokes with back to center of the circle and continue side stroke across (Fig. 5).
18. Push off and side overarm stroke to center; shark circle stunt and side overarm stroke across (Fig. 5).
19. Push off and take one side stroke, two side overarm, and one side stroke across.
20. Push off and take one combination stroke (arms of breast stroke with crawl kick) to center; surface dive and combination stroke across.
21. Push off and take one combination stroke (arms of breast stroke with crawl kick) to center; forward somersault and combination stroke across.
22. Elementary backstroke to center; back somersault and continue across on back.
23. Plunge dive across, going between swimmers who are treading water and holding hands with arms straight (Fig. 6).
24. Push off on back, take two elementary backstrokes to center; scoop slowly onto face and elementary crawl or dog paddle back to place.
25. Push off on face and crawl kick to center; lift head, double up, and scoop slowly onto back, fin back to place.
26. Push off on side, swim two side strokes to center; smoothly change to the other side during the second glide and side stroke back on that side.
27. Push off on side, swim side stroke beyond center; circle about the swimmer from the opposite side and continue back to the starting place.
28. Swim front crawl or breast stroke to center; surface dive, follow with dolphin, and back crawl or elementary backstroke to the starting place.
29. Front crawl to center; reverse direction and front crawl back to place.
30. Back crawl to center; reverse direction and back crawl back to place.

Fig. 6.   Arches

TEACHING HINTS FOR SYNCHRONIZING

So that the swimmers may hear the music as well as possible, and for the improvement of the stroke, emphasize these points. In the crawl stroke eliminate the splash of the kicking; have the hands cut the water at entry; keep the water, when exhaling, at nose level; do not roll the body. In other words, have the swimmers develop a smooth and quiet, though strong, stroke. With the elementary back, side, and breast strokes, see that the legs and arms do not come out of the water and that the recovery movements are smooth and easy. Pay particular heed to the points below for teaching swimming in unison.

1. Use percussive beats and waltz records to synchronize skills and accompaniment.
2. Pair off those swimmers whose abilities in a skill are comparable. Later, add a third and a fourth swimmer to the pair.
3. Choose one swimmer with particularly good control and rhythm as the leader with whom the others synchronize their strokes.
    a) In a horizontal line, the end swimmer is usually in the best position to be the leader and set the speed of the strokes.
    b) In a vertical line, the first swimmer is usually the leader.
4. Start swimmers across the pool, always using the same start for a given stroke. When they reach the other side, have them turn toward the shallow end of the pool unless otherwise desired.
5. Have crawl swimmers always start with the same arm when swimming lengths.
6. Have the swimmers keep their eye on the leader and out of the water. With some experience they can do this without turning the head too obviously.
7. Be sure the swimmers keep the position of the body steady; allow no roll.
8. Have the swimmers think of the position of their arms and legs so that all entry points of hands, recovery of arms, and use of legs are uniform.
9. Use admonitions and percussive means to help the leader, the pairs, and the group at any time they become irregular in their timing.

DEVELOPING STRENGTH, ENDURANCE, AND CONTROL

Check regularly the fundamental techniques of breathing, back float, sculling, and rolls. Ability to do them easily and with control develops a kinesthetic awareness of position and a lack of tension that is an asset to any swimmer. The rhythmic breathing should be done easily in an approximate ratio of two counts for inspiration and four for expiration with no holding of the breath at any time. Bobbing up and down fifty times successively in deep water with the body straight, using rhythmic breathing, builds endurance and minimizes tension. Swimmers also should practice holding varying volumes of air by exerting post-nasal pressure to prevent water entering the nose.

Teach stretched back float position with the tops of the legs and of the insteps at the surface of the water and eyes focusing on the feet. During the practice of the float, encourage the release of muscular tension in order to develop an easy position. Tipping the pelvis down flattens any arch in the back and helps raise and keep the legs at the horizontal level. To gain pelvic flexibility, which is essential for control, stand tall against the pool wall with heels about four inches from the wall: practice contracting the abdominal muscles to flatten the lower back against the wall and releasing them. In the back float position check the efficiency of the sculling movement as the swimmer sculls head first and feet first.

The head and shoulders are also very important in balancing the body and in directing movement. Make the swimmer aware of this as he glides on his side and when he rolls from the back float position onto the face and vice versa.

As the swimmers become proficient they can team up with other swimmers in tandem swimming, floating duets, joined lines in motion, somersault tandem—all of which are described in this book.

Endurance swimming for 220 yards with each stroke is an achievement for the swimmers and a good background for developing strength for continuous synchronized swimming. Synchronization of skills the length of the pool requires more strength and endurance than across the pool. Have the swimmers practice *singly* combinations of strokes and stunts the length of the pool, working for perfect *timing* with the *music;* then have them go in twos and threes working for perfect synchronization with each other. Suitable combinations are: two breast or two front crawl strokes followed by the porpoise or front somersault; two back crawl strokes or sculling followed by a dolphin or back somersault; two side, back, or front crawl strokes followed by a shark circle; and a standing dive with any of the strokes. Drill, drill, and more drill results in precision in execution.

Practice the standing dive to music. A standing dive takes four measures or a phrase of music. Start with the spring up from the edge of the pool; then dive into the water to the bottom and, with both hands leading, push up diagonally, onto the surface, ready to stroke on the accent of the fifth measure. An alternate way to emerge from the water is to push up onto the surface with one arm leading, ready to swing the other arm forward on the fifth measure. Aim for a definite marking on the bottom of the pool; learn to count the measures under water. Synchronize the dive with one diver following after a four measure interval—as soon as the first one dives into the water, the second one steps to the edge of the pool ready to spring up at the beginning of the next phrase. Synchronize the dive in twos, side by side. Learn to watch the partner under water.

SHORT ROUTINES

A short form of musical composition as described in Chapter 2 is a good guide for designing swimming routines across the pool. A study of *Routines A* (given below) demonstrates the basic principles of designing as discussed in Chapter 7 and gives an idea of proportion of parts to the whole. Teach one to the class that emphasizes a particular skill taught in class. Explain the composition of the routine and ask the members to suggest a different third or fourth part or an entirely different routine and bring out the good and weak points of their suggestions. Do not be discouraged if the suggestions are few as the students are inexperienced and may hesitate to express ideas. Many persons lack a strong rhythmic sense and know little about the prin-

ciples of good composition, but continual emphasis on the development of
these aspects brings worthwhile results.

The considerations in arranging these routines for the regular swimming
classes are as follows:

1. The routines should be simple. This is necessary for the inexperienced
   groups and, if the routines are well synchronized, they are effective even
   though they may not be intricate.
2. The number of swimmers should not be restricted.
3. The routines should be swum preferably across a 30-foot pool. This permits groups of varying sizes to participate. The turn at the wall gives a
   timely pause and provides a satisfactory length to each part of a routine.
4. Routines should be adaptable. In the following descriptions of routines,
   variations are suggested in the use of skills, patterns, and combinations of
   skills in the third part of a routine.
5. They should be conducted by the teacher. He stands in the center outside
   the shallow end of the pool. He anticipates the beginning of a phrase and
   gives the cue for each start across the pool, making sure that all swimmers
   are ready before doing so. He indicates the rhythm by percussive means or
   by a gesture if a record is played.

Routines A. In Routines 1-4 the swimmers start in the water along one side
of the pool, proceed back and forth across, and end up at the side again; in
routine 5 the swimmers start outside the pool.

1. Demonstrating Elementary Backstroke: weaving two horizontal lines.
   a) Push off on back with arms at side, synchronize the elementary backstroke including the glide across the pool. Turn toward the shallow end
   and take hold of the edge of the pool with both hands, ready to start
   again. Check position to be sure of being opposite a space (Fig. 3).
   b) Repeat *a* back across the pool. Turn toward the shallow end and get
   ready.
   c) Push off on back with arms at side, take two elementary backstrokes
   including the glide, start arms as in backstroke and make a big, slow
   scoop onto the face. Swim elementary crawl with a splash kick back to
   the starting place and hold on in a position of readiness again. This
   scoop occurs as the two lines form one line in the center (Fig. 4).
   d) Push off on back and synchronize elementary backstroke across.
   Variations:
   (1) Use one horizontal line for a pattern.
   (2) Use the dog paddle instead of the elementary crawl in *c*.
2. Demonstrating Crawl Kicks and Finning or Sculling.
   Back Crawl Kick: weaving two horizontal lines.
   a) Push off in two lines from opposite sides of the pool and synchronize
   back crawl kick.
   *b)*Synchronize finning with a little splash back across.
   c) Synchronize back crawl kick to center, roll over as the two lines pass
   each other, and elementary crawl across.
   d) Synchronize the finning, swelling the kick or splashing uniformly.
   Sculling: weaving two horizontal lines.

    a) Push off and scull across head first.

    b) Scull back across feet first.

    c) Scull head first to the center, scoop onto the face and front crawl kick back to the side.

    d) Back crawl kick with a swell across the pool.

        Variation: In *c* scull head first to the center, dolphin, and continue sculling across the pool.

Using a Kickboard: weaving two horizontal lines.

    a) Synchronize front crawl kick across.

    b) Synchronize front crawl kick with rhythmic breathing across.

    c) Synchronize scissors kick with one arm of the side stroke across.

    d) Synchronize front crawl kick with a swell.

3. Demonstrating Side and Side Overarm Strokes on the same side: one horizontal line.

    a) Synchronize side stroke across, swimming on the right side.

    b) Repeat *a* back across.

    c) Synchronize side stroke on the right side to center; describe a circle about six feet in diameter using four side strokes with back to center of small circle; continue side stroke to the other side (Fig. 5).

    d) Repeat *a* back across.

    Variations:

        (1) Use side overarm stroke instead of side stroke.

        (2) Swim *b* and *d* on the left side.

        (3) Use a weaving pattern of two horizontal lines in *a, b,* and *d;* but when describing the circle in *c,* one horizontal line synchronizes its circle first and then the other follows.

4. Demonstrating Crawl Strokes: weaving two horizontal lines.

    a) Synchronize front crawl stroke across the pool.

    b) Repeat *a* back across.

    c) Synchronize crawl stroke to center, roll onto back and take one arm pull of back crawl, roll onto face and take one front crawl pull, repeat the spiral, and continue with front crawl across.

    d) Repeat *a* across.

    Variations:

        (1) In *c* synchronize front crawl to center, roll onto back, and back crawl across.

        (2) In *c* reverse directions in the center and return to the starting position.

        (3) Substitute back crawl for front crawl and front crawl for back.

5. Demonstrating Porpoise: weaving two horizontal lines.

    a) Right horizontal line—synchronize a dive into the water and come up in the center of the pool, tread water, extend arms and join hands. Left horizontal line—synchronize a shallow dive, weaving through the line of treaders, and front crawl kick across (Fig. 6). Right horizontal line—synchronize breast stroke arm pull and crawl kick to the opposite side.

    b) Both lines—synchronize breast stroke arm pull and crawl kick across.

    c) Right line—synchronize one breast stroke arm pull and crawl kick combination to the center, on a second pull porpoise dive and come up together, repeat porpoise dive, and crawl kick across. Left line—follow doing the same skills.

d) Synchronize breast stroke arm pull and crawl kick with a splash across.
Variation: Substitute forward somersault for porpoise dive.

ROUTINES B. These routines are more difficult than Routines A because of the increased distance covered and because of the turns involved when changing directions. They all require that the swimmers be at home in deep water.

In all Routines B, the swimmers start from the end of the pool and proceed up the pool in two parallel vertical lines; go out to the sides, back and forth across the pool in horizontal lines, back to the center of the pool; and out in vertical lines.

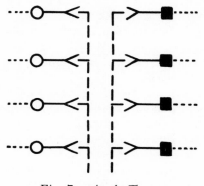

Fig. 7.   Angle Turns

1. Demonstrating the Side and Side Overarm Strokes on both sides.
   a) Two lines face each other and synchronize side stroke in two parallel vertical lines up the center of the pool. On signal, each line turns and swims side stroke to the sides of the pool (Fig. 7). The left line moves down the pool a few feet to be opposite a space. Hold onto the edge of the pool in readiness.
   b) Synchronize side stroke on the right side across.
   c) Synchronize side overarm stroke across the pool on the left side.
   d) Synchronize side stroke on the right side to just beyond center, make a right angle turn, and each line continues side stroke, facing each other but going in opposite directions to the ends of the pool (Fig. 8).
   Variation: For *c*—synchronize two side overarm strokes on the left side to the center; reverse on the last glide, and take three side overarm strokes on the right side back to place. For *d*—substitute side stroke on the left side.
2. Demonstrating the Crawl Strokes.
   a) Synchronize front crawl stroke up the center of the pool in two vertical lines, each couple starting two strokes after the preceding one. At the end of the pool turn out to the sides and down to the middle area of the pool (Fig. 9). Take hold with one hand, facing the shallow end, and extend the other out on the water in readiness.
   b) Synchronize front crawl across. Hold onto the edge with both hands ready to do back crawl.

    c) Synchronize back crawl across, starting with arm near the shollow end. Turn and be ready to do front crawl.

    d) Synchronize front crawl just beyond center, turn down pool, and continue to crawl in two lines to the end (Fig. 10).

    Variations:

    (1) Vary the entrance and exit patterns.

    (2) In *c* alternate front and back crawl strokes for the back crawl.

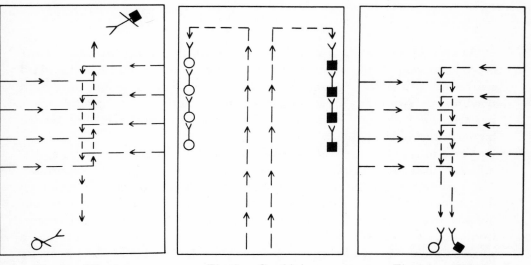

Fig. 8.   Weaving Horizontal and Vertical Lines

Fig. 9.   Combining Horizontal and Vertical Lines

Fig. 10.   Weaving Horizontal and Vertical Lines

ROUTINES C. These routines proceed down the length of the pool; the swimmers conduct their own timing. The skills synchronize with sixteen successive measures of music, which are repeated in each case.

    1. Demonstrating Breast Stroke.

        a) 8 measures: swim 4 breast strokes with the glide.

        b) 4 measures: swim 4 butterfly breast strokes.

        c) 4 measures: swim 2 breast strokes.

    2. Demonstrating Crawl Strokes.

        a) 12 measures: swim 6 front crawl strokes.

        b) 4 measures: swim 2 spiral strokes (1 front arm pull, 1 back, 1 front, and 1 back).

    3. Demonstrating Crawl Strokes and Stunts.

        a) 8 measures: swim 4 front crawl strokes, or 4 back crawl strokes.

        b) 4 measures: make 1 porpoise dive, or 1 somersault.

        c) 4 measures: swim 2 spiral strokes.

4

STROKES

As soon as the standard strokes are mastered, the synchronized swimmer is ready to vary them to interpret the mood of music or an idea. Standard strokes are principally for speed or utility while their variations as used in synchronized swimming are for design and beauty. One of the chief differences between the two types is that in the latter the head and arms are carried higher, causing the leg kick to be deeper.

Variations of the standard strokes increase the means of expressing the mood or idea of a composition and encourage individuality of expression. The variation might be the theme of a composition or a way of developing the theme; it might be a means of transition from one stunt to another, but the intriguing element of surprise in the unexpected movement or the direction of the movement in the stroke adds excitement and pleasure. These strokes should be repeated many times so that the spectators become aware of their significance in the over-all pattern.

Synchronized swimming groups have found certain modifications of strokes and hybrid combinations especially successful. Many are described and illustrated on the following pages and are examples of the unlimited possibilities for originating stroke variations. This opportunity to create makes synchronized swimming a fascinating activity for the swimmer with imagination and offers other swimmers new techniques to learn and master.

To assure that the swimmers execute the strokes properly, they must strive for smooth, effortless, controlled movement; continuity of movement; even rhythm; body balance with proper relaxation; regular and effortless breathing; good body alignment, especially in regard to keeping the head well back in line with the body; a pleasing line of hand and arm; and full body extension.

MODIFIED STROKES

Modified strokes vary from standard strokes in the movements and positions of the hands and arms. The difference occurs in the angle, direction, or timing of movements of the fingers, hand, wrist, lower arm, elbow, or upper arm. The action of the legs may vary as well as the position of the head or torso, but the coordination of arms and legs is usually the same as in the standard strokes.

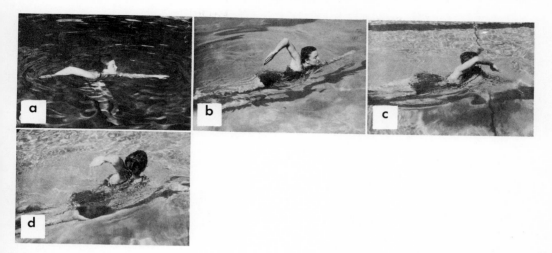

Plate 1

SYNCHRONIZED FRONT CRAWL

Plate 1	*Starting Position*	*Measure*

a   Left arm forward on water, right arm ready to lift on recovery.

Execution

b   Hold the head high out of the water, in a straight-ahead position. Do not turn the head from side to side.

Arm Action: Recover right arm with elbow held high and flexed at a ninety degree angle.

c   Turn the palm outward as the hand enters the water about twelve inches in front of the center of the face.   1

d   Straighten the arm and exert pressure downward and back, eliminating the standard forward reach. Keep the shoulders on a level plane.

Leg Action: Execute three deep flutter kicks on each arm pull when the arm movements are slow. Use two kicks if the arm movements are more rapid. *OR* execute one scissors kick on each arm pull, with a slight twist of the hips. Bring the same leg forward each time.

Repeat with the other arm.   2

The accent may come on the pull of the arm stroke, *or* on the elbow lift.

Plate 2

REVERSE TURN FOR FRONT CRAWL STROKE

This turn enables a crawl swimmer to reverse direction any place in the water smoothly and without losing the rhythm.

Plate 2	*Starting Position*	*Measure*
a	Extend the left arm forward ready to catch the water. The right arm is emerging from the water in the back.	

Execution

b	Pull part way with the left arm as the body turns toward the right, halfway around, facing in the opposite direction. Double up the legs and extend them in back to kick. Recover the right arm over the same area of water from which it just emerged.	1
c	Pull with the right arm at this spot, as the left arm recovers in the usual manner.	2

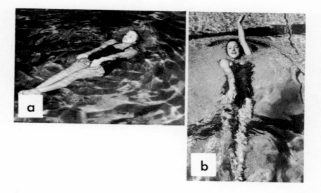

Plate 3

SYNCHRONIZED BACK CRAWL

Plate 3	*Starting Position*	*Measure*

a   Lie on back, both arms forward on the surface of the water, palms down.

Execution

Hold chin well in toward chest so that the head is in good alignment with the body.

b   *Arm Action:* Raise left arm so that hand enters the water above shoulder level. Pull gently with a straight left arm, hand just under the surface of the water. Keep the shoulders on a level plane.

Leg Action: Execute three deep flutter kicks on each arm pull when the arm pull is slow. Use two kicks if the arm pull is more rapid. *OR* execute two vertical scissors kicks on each arm pull separating the legs as in the usual scissors kick, except that one leg moves upward, the other downward. The same leg moves upward each time.   1

Repeat with other arm.   2

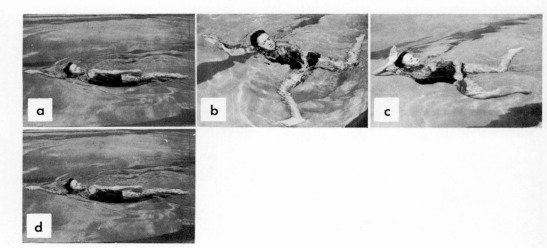

Plate 4

MODIFIED SIDE STROKE

Plate 4	Starting Position	Measure
a	Lie on side, top arm over hip, lower arm extended under head.	

Execution

b	Open the legs as the hands come toward each other.	1
c	Close the legs as the hand and wrist of the forward arm slip above the water close to the ear. See that the hand reaches high after it emerges from the water.	2
d	Return the forward hand to the water and assume the glide position of the side stroke.	3

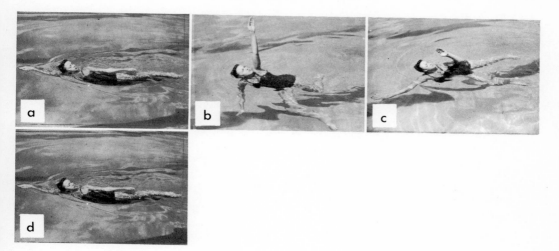

Plate 5

MODIFIED SIDE OVERARM STROKE I

Plate 5	*Starting Position*	*Measure*
a	Lie on side, top arm over hip, lower arm extended under head.	

Execution

b	Open the legs as the straight upper arm is brought out of the water to a position over the head.	1
c	Bend the elbow and bring the hand to the hip as the legs drive together.	2
d	The hand returns to the water as the body stretches to the glide position of the side stroke.	3

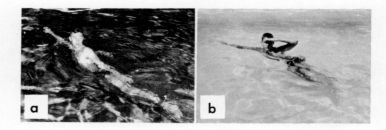

Plate 6

MODIFIED SIDE OVERARM STROKE II

| *Plate 6* | *Starting Position* | *Measure* |

a　　Lie on side, top arm over hip, lower arm extended under head.

Execution

Open the legs as the top hand is held to the forehead in a salute position and the lower arm recovers in the usual manner.

b　　Close the legs as the lower arm stretches to the glide position of the side stroke.　　　　　　　　　　　　　　　　1

Hold the salute for any desired number of bars, always with the top hand.

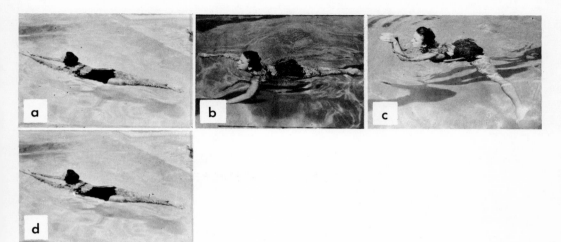

Plate 7

MODIFIED BREAST STROKE

Plate 7	*Starting Position*	*Measure*

a   Lie on stomach, extend both arms forward on the surface of the water.

Execution

b   Pull out to the sides with the arms. The legs open at the close of the arm pull.   1

c   Drive the legs together as hands recover in front of eyes, index fingers touching, fingers pointed upward until wrists pass the eyes. Bend the wrists to bring hands parallel to the surface of the water.

d   Extend arms forward to the glide position of the breast stroke.   2

Use the butterfly breast stroke for accent or for splashing effect.

Plate 8

MODIFIED BACKSTROKE I

Plate 8	*Starting Position*	*Measure*
a	Lie on back, extend both arms forward on the surface of the water, palms up.	

Execution

b	Slowly and evenly, raise both arms together to a position over the face, maintaining a strong leg kick.	1
c	Bend elbows slowly and return to the starting position.	2

Plate 9

MODIFIED BACKSTROKE II

Plate 9	*Starting Position*	*Measure*
a	Extend both arms forward on the surface of the water, palms up.	

Execution

b	Raise arms simultaneously forward to a position over the face, being careful to keep the arms straight during the entire execution.	1
c	Lower the arms sideward to the water at shoulder level and pull as in the elementary backstroke.	2

This stroke is especially effective in tandems.

HYBRID STROKES

A hybrid stroke combines parts of two or more standard strokes, such as a combination of breast stroke, side stroke, back crawl, and front crawl. Swimmers usually start a different stroke in the combination before they fully complete the previous one. For example, in Plate 10, the swimmer begins the arm pull of the breast stroke but rolls onto the right side for the start of the side stroke before completing the breast stroke arm pull.

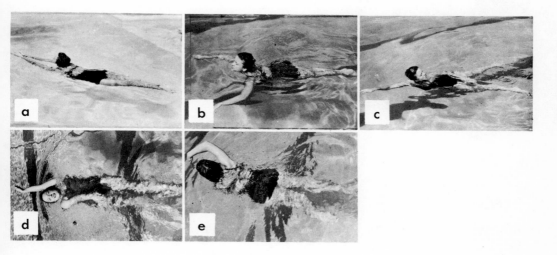

Plate 10

HYBRID—BREAST, SIDE, BACK CRAWL, FRONT CRAWL

Plate 10	*Starting Position*	*Measure*
a	Extend both arms forward on the surface of the water.	

Execution

b	Start the arm pull of the breast stroke. Continue to a half-pull position and roll onto the right side.	1
c	Drive the legs together as the arms stretch to a point just short of the glide position of the side stroke and roll onto the back.	2
d	Catch the water with the left arm on a back crawl pull and roll to the left onto the face.	3
e	Catch the water with the right arm on a front crawl pull.	4

Repeat the entire combination several times, maintaining the same tempo throughout.

The line of direction may be changed at any time during the execution of the hybrid.

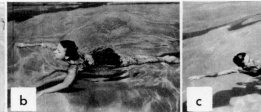

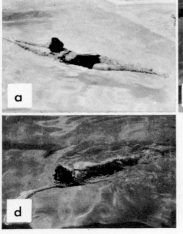

Plate 11

HYBRID—BREAST, SIDE, GLIDE

Plate 11	*Starting Position*	*Measure*
a	Extend both arms forward on the surface of the water.	

Execution

b, c	Start arm pull of breast stroke; continue to a half-pull position rolling onto right side in a diagonally forward direction to the right.	1
c, d	Drive the legs together as arms stretch to a point just short of the glide position of the side stroke. Shift onto the left side in a diagonally forward direction to the left.	2
	Drive the legs together as the right arm finishes its pull and both arms stretch to the complete glide position of the side stroke.	3
	Glide.	4

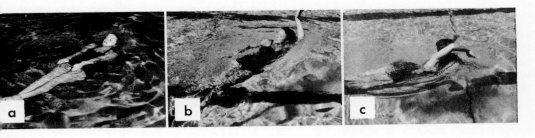

Plate 12

SPIRAL CRAWL

Plate 12	Starting Position	Measure
a	Lie on back, both arms forward on surface of the water, palms down.	

Execution

| b | Execute a back crawl stroke with the left arm, rolling to the left onto the face. | 1 |
| c | Execute a front crawl stroke with the right arm, rolling to the left onto the back. | 2 |

Continue, rolling in the same direction each time.

WALTZ CRAWL

The waltz crawl, strictly speaking, is not a hybrid, since one and one-half back crawl strokes are completed before the swimmer rolls onto her face for the front crawl strokes.

Plate 12	Starting Position	Measure
a	Lie on back, both arms forward on surface of the water, palms down.	
b	Execute one and one-half back crawl strokes, left arm, right arm, left arm, rolling to the left onto the face.	1-3
c	Execute one and one-half front crawl strokes, right arm, left arm, right arm, rolling to the left onto the back.	4-6

Continue, rolling in the same direction each time.

IN PAIRS

In pairs, swimmers may be unattached or attached. Unattached pairs swim in vertical, staggered, or horizontal lines. Swimmers join inside hands when swimming the crawl side by side, or use a tandem form for any stroke in which they progress in a line, one before the other. In tandem, swimmers may be connected in three ways: at the neck, under the arms, and at the waist.

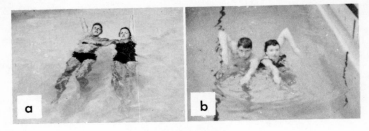

Plate 13

SWIMMING IN PAIRS SIDE BY SIDE

Plate 13   *Starting Position*

Tread water side by side.

Execution

a, b   Execute strokes simultaneously keeping heads in an even line.

Adapt the power of the arm pulls and the leg kicks to that of the weaker swimmer.

Try a staggered formation. It is similar to the above except that one person is slightly behind and to the side of the other.

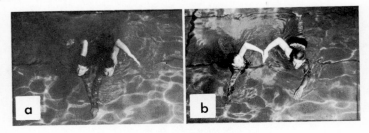

Plate 14

FRONT CRAWL WITH INSIDE HANDS JOINED

Plate 14   *Starting Position*

a   Inside hands joined, front crawl position.

Execution

b   Perform front crawl stroke, keeping shoulders on the same level and maintaining even arm pulls.

Plate 15

TANDEM

Plate 15

a   Connection at the neck, by hooking the feet on either side of the neck.

b   Connection under the arms, by hooking the feet, one under each arm.

c   Connection at the waist, by hooking the feet lightly around the waist, one on either side.

SEQUENCES OF STROKES

Strokes swum in various sequences are very effective. Try the various combinations of the front and back crawl, the short routine using the side or the side overarm, and the front crawl with the reverse turn—all described below.

FRONT AND BACK CRAWL COMBINATIONS. Change from front to back crawl and vice versa on the odd number of arm pulls, using the spiral turn. Changing in this sequence means that the turn is always made in the same direction, which keeps the swimming smooth. Vary the patterns. For instance, swim any sequence in horizontal and weaving lines, in diagonal and weaving diagonal lines (Figs. 11 and 12), or in vertical lines (Fig. 13). Start half the group with the right arm and half with the left. Or, start half the group with the front crawl and half with the back.

Combine the changes at odd intervals into this sequence: 5, 3, 1, 1, 3. In a horizontal line, start all the swimmers at the same time and have them stroke successively five front, three back, one front, one back, and three front; five back, three front, and so on. Try the sequence in a vertical line of three. Start all at the same time with the same arm but 1 starts with five front, continues three back, one front, and so on; 2 starts one front, continues one back, three front, and so on.

In this sequence, have the swimmers change every three arm pulls, but at first 1 takes four, then changes to back crawl and vice versa every three, while 2 changes every three from the beginning.

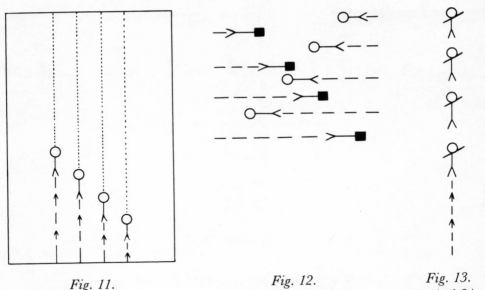

Fig. 11.
Diagonal Lines

Fig. 12.
Weaving Diagonal Lines

Fig. 13.
Vertical Line

SIDE OR SIDE OVERARM. Build a sequence of side or side overarm into a short routine. For example, have two swimmers, close together and facing each other, swim four strokes in the same direction. Reverse directions on the glide of the last stroke. Swim four strokes on the other side in the opposite direction and reverse. Swim two strokes and reverse; swim two more and reverse. Swim two strokes, hesitate, and somersault toward each other.

FRONT CRAWL AND REVERSE TURN. In a weaving pattern, repeat the front crawl stroke, a diminishing number of times after each turn. For instance, four swimmers start from each end of a 60-foot area. All synchronize fifteen front crawl arm pulls, weaving two horizontal lines; reverse directions. Then all synchronize nine pulls, weaving; reverse directions. All synchronize six pulls, weaving; reverse direction. All synchronize two pulls and tread water in one horizontal line. To vary this last part, have all continue swimming to their starting positions.

IMPROVISATIONS

The various rhythms and moods expressed in musical compositions are an excellent source for new and modified water techniques. Play swimmable music—a fox trot, blues song, tango, Latin rhythm, march, minuet or pavane —and have the swimmers experiment in the water. Preconceived ideas of the movement on land of most of the dance rhythms help guide the swimmers in their expression and their designing of patterns. Examples of improvisations using the bounce, the salute, the hesitation, the double-quick, the minuet, slapping the water, and turns follow.

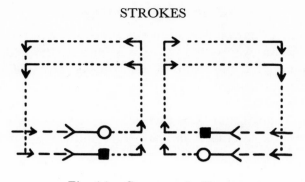

Fig. 14. Squares—the Bounce

THE BOUNCE. The effect of bouncing rhythmically over the surface of the
water is gained when a swimmer uses the trudgen with a single or double
scissors kick, accenting the lift of the elbow and shoulder, and the kick. "Sun-
rise Serenade," a slow fox trot in 4/4 time, played by Glenn Miller, inspires
this bounce. The tempo is twenty-two bars to a minute. Make two elbow
lifts in one measure, on the primary and secondary accents. A blues, such as
"St. Louis Blues," is also suitable for bouncing. The swimmers should feel
the syncopated rhythm, exaggerate the elbow lift, and jerk the kick to produce the bouncing effect. This is a decided contrast to the smooth crawl stroke.

Use the bounce in a pattern. Have couples 1 and 2 each describe a square,
starting at the same time and from opposite sides of the pool (Fig. 14). Square
the corners with sharp right and left angle turns. Swim two front strokes side
by side toward center; make angle turns up the pool. Swim two back strokes
in single file up the pool; turn toward the starting side. Then swim two front
strokes side by side toward the pool side; turn down the pool. Finally swim
two back strokes in single file down the pool to the starting position.

The bounce is an excellent take-off stroke for a comedy act. A sharp turn
with an exaggerated arm swing fits the humorous mood. If going to the right,
stroke with the right arm, make a right angle turn and swing the left arm
three-quarters the way around to stroke in the new direction, using a jerky
kick.

THE SALUTE. Use march music, 4/4 time, such as "Anchors Aweigh" and
"The Marine Hymn," for the salute. Practice a clean cut, precise arm movement by accenting the lift of the arm as it begins its recovery in either the
front or back crawl stroke. Salute momentarily with the right hand during
the arm recovery on the secondary accent of the measure, indicated by *and*
in the following example:

Measure 1: Stroke with the right arm; recover the left.
Measure 2: Stroke with the left arm; recover the right.
Measure 3: Stroke with the right; recover the left.
Measure 4: Start arm recovery of the right; stroke with the left;
   and salute with the right hand; complete stroking with the left.

A short routine of sixteen bars in march time follows:

4 measures: Swim two front crawl strokes, starting the pull with the right arm on measure 1 and saluting with the right on *and* of measure 4.

4 measures: Repeat, continuing in the same direction.

4 measures: Repeat.

4 measures: Tread water. Use two vertical scissors kicks to pop the swimmer up on each kick and turn him halfway around. Hold the salute throughout.

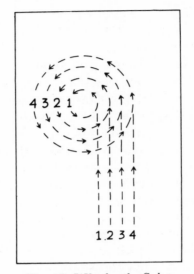

Fig. 15. Wheel—the Salute

The following excerpt from a water composition uses the salute in a wheel pattern (Fig. 15). Four swimmers stand abreast, facing up the pool and saluting.

8 measures: All swim four front crawl strokes up the pool, starting with the right arm.

24 measures: With 1 as the hub, all swim twelve front crawl strokes in a wheel pattern one and a half times around. Salute with the right hand during every fourth measure,

4 measures. All tread water using scissors kick to pop up two times. Hold the salute.

4 measures: Each salutes and faces right about in turn on each succeeding measure of music.

THE HESITATION. Use a waltz or a smooth fox trot with one back crawl arm pull to a measure of music. In this number swim the back crawl with a straight elbow, raising the arm straight up and over the shoulder on recovery.

Measure 1: Lift right arm up and over the shoulder; pull left arm to the side.

Measure 2: Pull right arm to the side; lift left arm.

Measure 3: Life right arm to touch the water in back; pull left arm to the side.

Measure 4: Instead of pulling the right arm, retrace the air path of the right back to the starting position; hold left arm at the side.

Measure 5: Hold right arm at the side; lift the left over head.

Measure 6: Life right arm; pull left arm to the side.

Measure 7: Pull right arm; lift the left.

Measure 8: Hold right arm to the side; retrace the air path of the left.

THE DOUBLE-QUICK STROKE. Double-quick means that the swimmer takes two short crawl arm pulls in the usual time for one pull. Experimenting to tango music produced this stroke modification and led to many variations of it. The tango, "Jalousie," 2/4 time, in Columbia album C-90, has thirty-two bars to a minute at middle tempo; one regular arm pull is taken to a measure. This tempo requires a slow, smooth stroke and allows time for a double-quick movement. An example of a four bar phrase follows:

Measure 1: Stroke with the left.

Measure 2: Stroke with the right.

Measure 3: Stroke with the left.

Measure 4: One double-quick stroke—take one short pull with the right followed by one with the left. (Feel the music; it suggests the exact timing.)

Repeat the 4 measures: Immediately start to stroke with the right.

The double-quick stroke may be done

1. Forward and backward: on measure 4 take a short crawl pull in front with the right followed by a short crawl pull in back of the swimmer with the left.
2. To both sides: on measure 4 take a short crawl pull to the right side with the right arm followed by a short pull to the left side with the left.
3. In a spiral: on measure 4 take a short crawl pull forward with the right, rolling onto the back; follow with a short back crawl pull with the left, rolling onto the face; on measure 1 take a regular front crawl pull forward with the right.
4. Using back crawl instead of front crawl.
5. In succession: take two double-quick strokes in succession progressing forward on measures 3 and 4.
6. In a reverse combination: take two double-quick strokes on measures 1 and 2, followed by a complete spiral in the regular tempo on measures 3 and 4.

THE MINUET. Beethoven's "Minuet in G," 3/4 time, as played on Victor record 1434, is slow and stately. There are thirty bars to a minute when played at a tempo slightly faster than middle; one arm pull uses one measure. The slow tempo allows for the following modification of the crawl during the fourth measure of a phrase.

Measure 1: Stroke with the right arm.

Measure 2: Stroke with the left arm.

Measure 3: Stroke with the right.

Measure 4: Hold the left arm in front for two beats of the measure; on the third beat make a short quick pull with the left, bringing the elbow out of the water and recovering the arm above the water; scull downward slightly with the right. This movement accents the third beat of the measure and syncopates the measure.

Repeat the 4 measures, starting with the left arm.

This rhythmic pattern in the water—*stroke, stroke, stroke, hold*—is analogous to one of the typical minuet steps—*step, step, step, point.*

The following is a water adaptation of a minuet figure involving four swimmers and swum across a 30-foot area. It synchronizes with the last sixteen measures of the "Minuet in G." Use the *stroke, stroke, stroke, hold* pattern during the first four measures. Start with two swimmers on each side of the 30-foot area, a few feet apart and each opposite a space. Use the weaving pattern.

4 measures: Swim 2 front crawl strokes to the center.

4 measures: Continue with one more front crawl stroke passing left shoulder, reverse direction, take 1 front crawl stroke, ending facing partner. Both tread water in the center of the 30-foot area, touching right hands high above the water.

4 measures: The man appears to turn the girl under his arm twice, using 2 measures for one complete turn. The girl turns herself by sculling with one hand.

4 measures: All take 2 back crawl strokes to the side opposite to the one from which each started.

Slapping the Water. The swimmers can make rhythmic percussive sounds by slapping the water. Take three front crawl pulls, lift the arm up in back and slap the water. Lower the legs and turn to look at the slap; the other arm quietly pulls part way for support. This is effective with the swimmers in horizontal, vertical or snake-like lines.

Turns in a Vertical Position. Certain phrases in a musical composition, usually at the end of a section of the music or during a transition part, suggest ideas for improvising water techniques involving turns. Turns offer interest and variety, help to develop climax, and give a conclusive note to the composition. There are many ways to do effective turns, depending upon the rhythm and mood of the music. A few suggestions follow for a swimmer treading water with one or both hands free for sculling and other movements.

(1) Turn the body around slowly or quickly. (2) Bounce up and down. (3) Slap the water in rapid succession—turning or not. (4) Swish the water horizontally with one arm. (5) Carry an arm in the air during the turn. (6) Effect a sustained movement.

TRANSITIONS

Changing from one stroke to another, from a stroke to a stunt, from one stunt to another, from a stunt to a stroke, or changing from one water skill to another should, except in special cases, be done smoothly and continuously with no stops. Swimming a few strokes, stopping, sculling, executing a stunt, stopping, chops up the swimming routine. It is better to select a sequence of skills that afford easy transitions— which means that the end of one skill leaves the swimmer in the correct position to continue into the next one, synchronizing each swimming movement with the underlying beat and phrasing of the music.

Examples of easy transitions from strokes to stunts are: (1) A shark stunt follows the front crawl, back crawl, and side strokes smoothly—pull back crawl left, right, left, right; leave the left arm above the head; roll onto the right side and start the shark; the left arm is already in shark position. This sequence makes a simple transition with rhythmic continuity. (2) Similarly continue smoothly from the shark stunt into the back crawl, front crawl, and side strokes. (3) Go into the porpoise stunt from the front crawl—pull front crawl right, left, right; leave left arm under water in front of the body until the right arm comes forward; proceed into a porpoise dive. (4) Go into a dolphin from the back crawl stroke—pull back crawl right, left, right; leave the left arm in back of the head until the right arm recovers and continue into the dolphin. (5) A survey of the starting position of each stunt in Chapter 5 will reveal others that can follow these strokes smoothly, such as going from the back crawl stroke into the barracuda, back pike somersault.

Examples of easy transitions from one stunt to another are: (1) swordfish into torpedo into a foot first dolphin; (2) shark into a dolphin; (3) ballet legs into a submarine; (4) porpoise into a flying dolphin or a flying porpoise; (5) ballet legs into a kip or flamingo; (6) front walk over into torpedo into foot first dolphin; (7) ballet legs into barracuda; (8) log roll, ending on the back, into a ballet leg type stunt, kip, or flamingo; (9) log roll, ending on the face, into a porpoise or front walk over; (10) ballet legs into a tub and vice versa or into a marlin and vice versa; (11) foot first dolphin into a marlin or tub.

The marlin is an excellent stunt with which to change body position and both the marlin and tub afford an easy change of direction; both also combine well with numerous stunts. One can come up into any direction from under the water—push up head first onto the back, front, or side and continue into a stunt, such as into the water wheel from the side position; or scull up feet first onto the back if the body is under water in a head down vertical position.

5

STUNTS

Stunts are a valuable unit in any swimming program and an integral part of a synchronized swimming program. No other area in swimming contributes more toward helping an individual become at home in the water. Stunts are self-testing activities which may be practiced alone or in groups. The student may progress as his readiness permits.

The instructor must see that the student develops balance, breath control, and neuro-muscular coordination. Without these he will be unable to progress in the field. Balance is the ability to maintain equilibrium even though the head, legs, or arms continually change position. Breath control in underwater work is gained as the swimmer learns to exert sufficient positive pressure in the post-nasal area to prevent water from entering the nose. All inhalation is, of course, through the mouth. Neuro-muscular coordination is attained when nerves and muscles are trained to work together to determine the amount and speed of muscular action to be used in the performance of a given stunt.

The inexperienced synchronized swimmer practices on simple stunts to develop balance, direction, timing, and controlled breathing. He endeavors to execute the stunts smoothly. He avoids exhaling under water since it produces bubbles. He strives to acquire good form through full body extension with the legs straight and together, toes pointed, tucks and pikes tight, vertical stunts strictly vertical, horizontal stunts horizontal, and dolphin type stunts following the circumference of a circle. As he becomes more proficient, he learns to execute the difficult stunts, working continually to attain smooth, controlled flowing movement which appears effortless.

A large repertory of stunts is desirable for both the beginning and the advanced student of synchronized swimming. It broadens the field of enjoyment and makes possible the creation of a more interesting and beautiful choreography.

To execute a stunt well, be sure to keep movements smooth, controlled, and flowing. See that the recovery movements are relaxed and easy. Avoid *drag* in any part of the stunt. Remember that jerky, uneven movements cause splashes. Strive for an execution which appears effortless. Always maintain good body alignment. Check on the position of the head. Control the breathing (lack of control results in bubbles and gasps). Execute the stunt in proper

rhythm. (To synchronize the stunts with rhythmic accompaniment, check the analysis and description of the stunt for the number of measures required, using 3/4 rhythm, for each separate operation in the stunt.)

The ability to scull properly cannot be overemphasized in synchronized swimming. Learn how to scull before attempting to execute any stunt because a swimmer can have no controlled movement or balance without this important technique.

Plate 16

SCULLING

Sculling may be executed in place, traveling toward the head, traveling toward the feet, or used in making turns, depending upon where the swimmer exerts the pressure with the hands.

Plate 16	*Starting Position*	*Measure*
a	*Surface Shot*	
	Lie on back, body extended, hands at hips.	
b, c	*Under Water Shots* showing hand action.	

Execution

b	Push hands away from body, palms turned outward, little fingers up.	1
c	Return hands toward body, palms turned inward, little fingers down.	2

Describe a figure eight with each hand during one complete sculling movement. Keep wrists pliable. Keep fingers relaxed.

Sculling is more effective if fingers are normal and relaxed. When the fingers are separated there is more surface tension than when they are together.

To Travel Toward the Head: As the hands move inward, flex wrists slightly with fingers pointing diagonally down and press water in and toward the feet. As the hands move outward, flex the wrists slightly with fingers pointing diagonally upward and press water out and toward the feet.

To Travel Toward the Feet: As the hands move inward with fingers pointing diagonally downward, press the water in and toward the head. As the hands move outward, flex the wrists slightly with little fingers upward and press the water out and toward the head.

To Turn to the Right: The right hand sculls, pressing the water inward and outward toward the feet. The left hand sculls with a reverse action, pressing the water inward and outward away from the feet.

To Stay in Place: Describe a figure eight with each hand. Exert equal pressure on both outward and inward pushes. Pressure is exerted downward rather than toward the feet or head.

Plate 17

Plate 17

a   For progessive practice in sculling, draw the right knee toward the chest, placing the foot against the inside of the left knee. Hold the left leg extended with toes on surface of the water. Travel toward the head or toward the feet.

b   Practice sculling for the purposes of turning, by drawing both knees toward the chest, keeping the tops of the feet on the surface of the water, and turning in place, first to the right and then to the left.

Teaching Hints

Do not allow finning which is movement consisting of little fingers following side of suit to the top of the hip bone, followed by the palms pushing toward the feet. This is a close-to-the-surface forward and back movement. Do not allow a frantic pawing up and down movement to which beginners often resort when they start to sink.

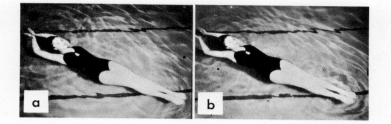

Plate 18

SCULLING ABOVE THE HEAD

Plate 18   *Starting Position*

Lie on back, body extended, legs together and straight, toes pointed, arms extended above the head.

Execution

a   Travel toward the feet by turning the palms outward and pushing the water upward away from the head. Separate the hands no more than the width of the shoulders, keeping elbows relaxed and straight. Keep the feet close to the surface of the water.

b   Turn the palms inward and push the water way from the head.

Describe a figure eight with each hand, exerting equal pressure on both outward and inward pushes.

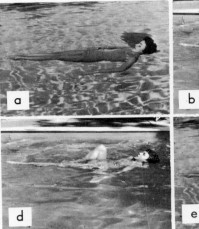
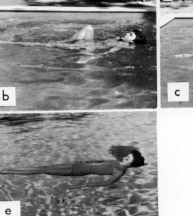

Plate 19

BALLET LEGS, SINGLE

Plate 19	*Starting Position*	*Measure*

a   Lie on back, body extended, hands at hips.

Execution

Scull continuously with the hands near the hips.

b   Bring the right knee toward the chest, drawing side of right foot along inside of extended leg, until the thigh is perpendicular to the surface of the water. (The knee does not move toward the chest during the remainder of the execution of the ballet leg.) Keep the left leg extended and motionless with toes at surface of water.   1

c   Straighten the right knee so that the entire leg is perpendicular to the surface of the water. Height is important.   2

d   Return to the bent knee position.   3

e   Slide the right foot along the inside of the extended leg as the leg returns to the starting position. Keep face above surface of water during entire execution.   4

Repeat with the left leg.

Traveling may occur at any time during the execution of the stunt.

Teaching Hints

Try focusing the eyes on the instep of the foot of the ballet leg during the execution.

Do not allow hips to drop low in the water.

Emphasize importance of continued forceful sculling as the ballet leg assumes the extended position. Beginners frequently cease to scull properly at this point. They change to a pawing movement with the hands which causes them to sink.

Emphasize good body alignment, including position of head.

To improve full extension of the knee of the ballet leg, push the heel upward, before extending the ankle.

Ballet legs are more easily learned at an early age before the hips and legs become heavier.

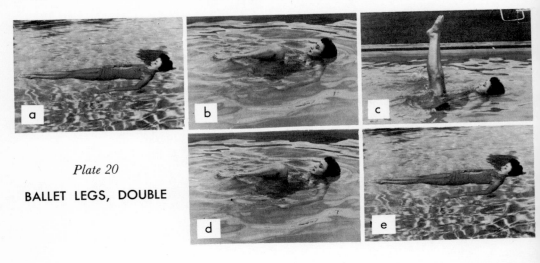

Plate 20

BALLET LEGS, DOUBLE

| *Plate 20* | *Starting Position* | *Measure* |

a   Lie on back, body extended, hands at hips.

Execution

Scull fast and forcefully with hands near hips.

b   Bring both knees simultaneously toward the chest until the thighs are perpendicular to the surface of the water. (The knees do not move toward the chest during the remainder of the execution of the stunt.)   1

c   Straighten both legs simultaneously so that they are perpendicular to the surface of the water. Focus the eyes on the knees.   2

d   Return to the bent knee position.   3

e   Resume starting position. Keep face above surface of water at all times.   4

Traveling may occur at any time during the execution of the stunt.

Teaching Hints

Keep the hips as high as possible in the water.

The water line on the vertical legs should be near mid-point on the thighs.

Emphasize the importance of continued forceful sculling, especially as the legs extend vertically.

Tighten abdominal muscles during extension of the legs.

A land practice exercise for strengthening these muscles is: Lie on the back and slowly lift both legs to the vertical and lower them slowly. Keep the knees straight.

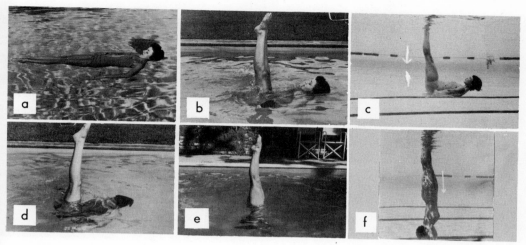

Plate 21

BARRACUDA

Plate 21	*Starting Position*	*Measure*
a	Lie on back, body extended, hands near hips.	

Execution

b Raise both legs rapidly to the vertical. 1

c Holding this position, submerge body no lower than ankles. 2

d With continuous sculling motion, raise the body until the water level is between the knees and the hips, with the face just under the surface of the water. 3-4

e Drop the trunk to the vertical position and thrust the legs vertically upward. In assuming the vertical position, straighten the lower back first and continue straightening the spine, with the head coming last into line. (To negotiate the drop of the trunk to the vertical and the thrust of the legs, press downward as far as possible with the arms, then rotate them outward at the shoulder joint and scoop the water until the arms finish above the head.) 5

f Submerge (drop). 6

Practice Hints

Try for no perceptible pause between body submergence and rise (c, d). Avoid excessive arch in the back by straightening body properly (e).

A barracuda may also be started from a layout position on the face. Execute a forward pike somersault* to the point at which the legs become vertical, then execute as in barracuda above (d, e, f).

*Somersault, Forward Pike, page 92.

Plate 22

BARRACUDA, SPINNING

Plate 22	Starting Position	Measure

a   Lie on back, body extended, hands at hips.

Execution

b, c, d, e Execute a barracuda to the height of the thrust.   1-4

f   Execute a fast turn of the body at least 180 degrees to the right, at the height of the thrust, in one quick movement by employing a forceful turn of the arms and shoulders. Whip left arm across in front of the face and the right arm toward the back of the head. As soon as the left arm whips across in front of the face, push it back to the left against the water to help with the spin. Hold the right arm for balance and scull with the right hand to keep the body high.   5

g   Submerge (drop).   6

Teaching Hints

The spin occurs at the top of the lift and is negotiated by arm and shoulder movements, not by head or hips. See that the body, fully extended, spins on its central axis. For variation, continue the spin during the entire period the body is dropping.

Plate 23
BARRACUDA,
BACK PIKE SOMERSAULT

Plate 23	*Starting Position*	*Measure*
a	Lie on back, body extended, hands at hips.	

Execution

b	Execute a back pike somersault (page 90) to the point at which the legs become vertical.	1-4
c	With continuous motion, raise the body by means of sculling, until the water level is between the hips and the knees with the face just under the surface of the water.	5-6
d	Drop the trunk to the vertical and thrust the legs vertically upward as high as possible. In assuming the vertical position, straighten the lower back first, continue straightening the spine through the cervical area, bringing the head into line last. (To negotiate the drop of the trunk to the vertical and the thrust of the legs, press downward as far as possible with the arms, then rotate them outward at the shoulder joint. Scoop the water until arms finish above head.)	7
e	Submerge (drop).	8

Teaching Hints

See that the body does not drop as the somersault is started on the surface of the water. Rotation starts immediately. The feet travel backward above the surface of the water as the somersault is started.

The movement during the entire execution of the stunt is continuous.

For rotation of the body, use big circular arm movements, described in the back pike somersault (see page 90), followed by powerful sculling as the body is rising, to obtain the greatest possible lift.

BARRACUDA, BACK PIKE SOMERSAULT, SPINNING*

The spin of at least 180 degrees occurs at the height of the lift.

For variation continue the spin during the entire period the body is dropping.

Plate 24

BARRACUDA, VARIATION

Plate 24	*Starting Position*	*Measure*
a	Lie on back, one knee bent, hands near hips.	
b	Maintain the bent knee position throughout the execution of a barracuda, back pike somersault,† until after the vertical thrust of the legs.	1-7
c	Straighten the bent knee before submergence of the ankles.	8

The bent knee variation may be used in any of the barracudas.

*Barracuda, Spinning, page 50.
†Barracuda, Back Pike Somersault, page 51.

Plate 25

CORKSCREW

| *Plate 25* | *Starting Position* | *Measure* |

a   Lie on right side, right arm extended under the head, left arm extended over hip in line with the body.

Execution

Roll toward the face by turning the head to the right and pressing backward with the right shoulder. Execute one complete revolution, holding the original extended position of the body, with no bend at hips or knees.   1-2

Plate 26

CATALINA

Plate 26	*Starting Position*	*Measure*

a   Assume a right ballet leg position.

Execution

b   Holding the ballet leg extended, rotate the body to the left to a face down position and at the same time pike the body sharply toward the left knee. As the body starts to rotate, the right hand moves toward the face. As the head moves downward beneath the hips, the right arm sweeps forcefully across the body past the right hip. Focus the eyes on the left hip. Left leg remains horizontal at water level.   1-2

c, d   Bring the left leg, which is still parallel to surface of the water, to meet vertical right leg before submergence of ankles.   3

e   Submerge (drop).   4

Practice Hints

For orientation, lie on back, legs together and straight, turn over to a face down position, bend sharply at hips, lift legs to vertical position and drop.

Have a helper hold foot of swimmer's vertical leg while swimmer practices rotating the hips and piking forward. Practice the same, holding foot of swimmer's horizontal leg.

The rotation in the hip during the roll-over at the start of the stunt is a quick movement. Practice this movement on the deck by standing on left leg, right leg extended forward at hip. Holding right leg in this position, pivot to the left on toe of left foot to face in opposite direction.

Teaching Hints

The right leg remains vertical during hip rotation. The foot should not travel in a circle. Ballet leg must pivot in hip joint to remain vertical. Do not bend the horizontal left knee during the rotation and pike. Hold the chin in normal position.

The right hand moves toward the face as the body first starts to rotate left, so that it will be in a position for its forceful sweep across the body.

Plate 27

CATALINA REVERSE

Plate 27	*Starting Position*	*Measure*
a	Lie on face, body extended, hands near hips.	

Execution

b	Execute a porpoise (page 85) to the vertical position.	1-2
c	Lower the left leg to a horizontal position on the surface of the water in front of the body.	3
c, d	Maintaining the vertical position of the right leg and the horizontal position of the left leg, execute a vigorous twist of the hips to the right as the trunk rises from the vertical position to the horizontal position on the back. (The left leg remains horizontal, the right leg vertical throughout the entire execution of the stunt.)	4
e	Surface the body in this position.	5-6
f	Finish in a layout position on the back.	7-8

The stunt may also be started from a layout position on the back, executing a kip (page 78) to the vertical position of Fig. 27b.

Plate 28

CRANE

Plate 28	*Starting Position*	*Measure*
a	Assume a right ballet leg position.	

Execution

b   Holding the ballet leg extended, lower the body backward until it is in vertical position, carrying the ballet leg over to a horizontal position, under the surface of the water, and raising the left leg to the vertical position, with the water line near upper calf. (The legs form a right angle with each other, not a "Y".) Keep the back straight.   1

c   Execute a half turn of the body in this position, with the head acting as a pivot. The ballet leg executes a half circle under the surface of the water.   2-3-4

d   After completion of this half turn, bring ballet leg up to meet the vertical leg.   5

e   Execute a half twist*. The water level on the legs remains stationary throughout the turn and twist.   6-7-8

f   With no drop, keep the knees straight and start to lay the feet on the surface of the water as the body is propelled to

*Twist, page 104.

the surface, feet first, by an overhead sculling movement of the hands.   9-10

g   Surface in a layout position on the back with feet pointing in the same direction as in the starting position.   11-12

Plate 29

DOLPHIN

Plate 29   *Starting Position*   *Measure*

a   Lie on back, body extended, hands at sides.

Execution

A dolphin follows the path of the circumference of a circle, the approximate diameter of which is often seven or eight feet.

b   Hold the body in good alignment, chin in normal position, body fully extended. *Pull* the body around the circle, either by means of sculling or by arm pulls. (As the body starts outward and downward the hands are above shoulder level and to the side rather than back of the head.) Have the feet follow the surface of the water until they disappear under water; they neither rise above nor depress below the surface.

c   Continue pulling the body around the circle with head and feet following the same path. Scull with hands at hips.

d   As the body rises, scull with the hands near the hips.

e   Return to the surface head first.   1-8

Practice Hints

In starting a dolphin, do not thrust the head back sharply and arch the back in order to get down. This causes the feet to rise above the surface of the water and makes an imperfect circle.

In surfacing, do not allow the head to pop up out of the water. This indicates that the swimmer has not made a complete circle.

Do not cut off any part of the circle.

During the entire execution, feel as though the hips are being pulled around the circle by means of the hands and arms.

Finish the dolphin in the same place in which it was started. Avoid a loop.

Plate 30

DOLPHIN, BALLET LEG

Plate 30	*Starting Position*	*Measure*
a	Assume the extended right ballet leg position.	

Execution

Start backward as in a dolphin,* holding ballet leg position.

b   The left leg meets the ballet leg just before submergence of feet. Ballet leg does not move back to meet left leg.

c, d, e   Continue around the circle and surface as in a dolphin.*   1-8

*Dolphin, page 57.

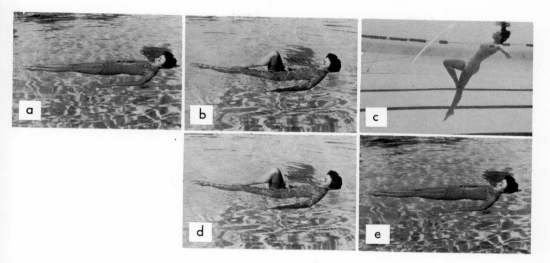

Plate 31

DOLPHIN, BENT KNEE

Plate 31	*Starting Position*	*Measure*

a   Lie on back, body extended, hands near hips.

Execution

b   Draw right knee toward chest until right foot is beside left knee.

c   Hold the foot to knee position and execute a dolphin (picture illustrates latter part of dolphin circle).

d   Hold bent knee until after surfacing.

e   Return bent knee to original starting position.   1-8

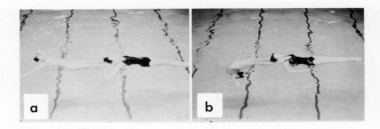

Plate 32

DOLPHIN, CHAIN

Plate 32	*Starting Position*	*Measure*

a   Two persons lie on back, one behind the other, connected by means of feet at the neck.

Execution

b   1 (the boy in this picture) starts a dolphin and pulls 2 to 1's former position to start her dolphin. The arms of each person continue pulling in unison until both have completed the dolphins and returned to the starting position. The connection is maintained during the entire execution.   1-10

Additional persons may be included in the chain. The one who starts the dolphin should travel under the surface of the water as far as the original position of the feet of the last person in the chain.

Plate 33

DOLPHIN, PINWHEEL

Plate 33	*Starting Position*	*Measure*
a	Two persons lie on back, one behind the other, connected by means of feet at the neck. The girl in this picture is 1.	

Execution

a	Start as in a dolphin, chain (Plate 32).	1-6
	1 makes a connection with the feet of 2 at the time 1's head breaks the surface of the water as she comes up.	7
b	Complete one revolution of the wheel before the connection is broken.	8-10
c	Return to starting position.	11-14

Additional persons may be included in the chain.

Several revolutions of the wheel may be executed before the connection is broken.

Teaching Hints

Breathing takes place as the faces pass over the surface of the water.
The arm pulls are stronger and faster than in the dolphin, chain.

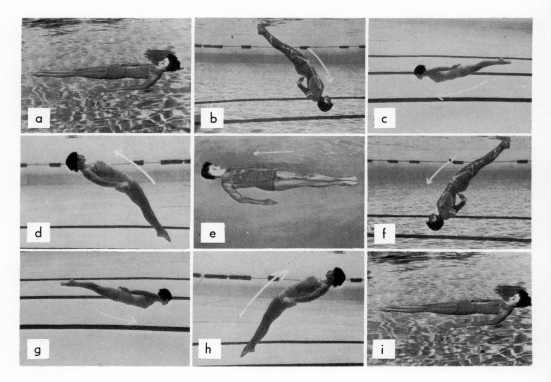

Plate 34

DOLPHIN, FIGURE EIGHT

Plate 34	*Starting Position*	*Measure*
a	Lie on back, body extended, legs together, hands at sides.	

Execution

b	Start a dolphin.*	1
c	Continue halfway around the circle.	2-3
d	Execute a half roll of the body before the surface is reached.	4
e	Return to the surface on back, facing in the opposite direction from which the start was made.	5-6
f	Immediately start another dolphin from this spot.	7
g	Continue halfway around the circle.	8-9
h	Repeat the half roll of the body before the surface is reached.	10
i	Return to the original starting position. A figure eight has been completed.	11, 12

*Dolphin, page 57.

Plate 35

DOLPHIN, FLYING

Plate 35	*Starting Position*	*Measure*

Stand on bottom of pool in water of a depth of two to four feet, arms at sides.

Execution

	Bend knees slightly, arms downward and back of body, ready to help start the lift.	1
	Push off from bottom of pool as arms swing forward and upward.	2
a	Drive the body high out of the water and execute a dolphin at the top of the lift.	3-6

Plate 36

DOLPHIN, FLYING, DOUBLE

Plate 36	*Starting Position*	*Measure*
	2 (the boy) stands on bottom of pool, knees bent, holding the feet of 1 in his hands.	
	Execution	
	2 lifts 1, as 1 springs upward as much as possible.	1
a	1 starts a flying dolphin at the top of the lift and completes it in the water.	
b	2 immediately executes a flying dolphin.	2-4

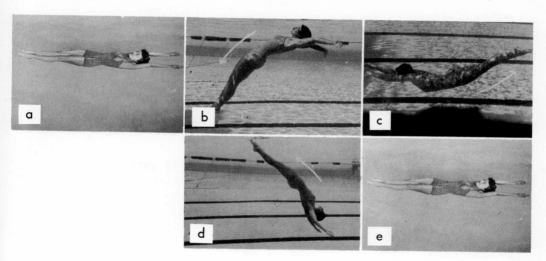

Plate 37

DOLPHIN, FOOT FIRST

Plate 37	*Starting Position*	*Measure*
a	Lie on back, body extended, arms overhead.	

Execution

b   By means of overhead sculling, force the feet and legs forward and outward along the path of a circle, the diameter of which is about eight feet. In order to follow the path of the circle, press downward with the feet and backward with fully extended legs and thighs. As the head with chin in normal position is ready to travel beneath the surface of the water, quickly slice the hands to the sides at shoulder level and scoop the water upward with two or three small scoops. (The entire movement is continuous.)   1-4

c   Slide the hands to the hips and press forcefully upward in front of the face, as far as possible, several times.   5-8

d   As the feet approach the top of the circle, scull gently overhead; the body follows the path of the circle and glides to the surface. Just before surfacing, straighten the back; little or no sculling is necessary.   9-10

e   Feet follow surface of water as body surfaces on the back.   11-12

Teaching Hints

Avoid a shallow path. Do not cut off any part of the circle.
See that the body is fully extended during the entire execution.
Avoid a hesitation just before the head drops below the surface of the

water. This is usually due to slow transition of arms from overhead to sides of shoulders. The hands should cut through the water with little resistance.

As the body surfaces, do not pike or the body will submerge; do not arch or feet will start down again. Keep back straight.

Finish the dolphin in the same place in which is was started. Avoid a loop.

Practice Hints

To acquire the kinesthetic sense of traveling feet first around a dolphin circle, stand on hands in shallow water, push against bottom of pool, and float up on the back; instruct swimmer in deep water to travel as far as he is able on the path of the dolphin circle and have an assistant pull him around the remainder of the circle.

The fundamental techniques for the foot first dolphin apply to its variations. To eliminate repetition, only information specific to each of its variations will be mentioned.

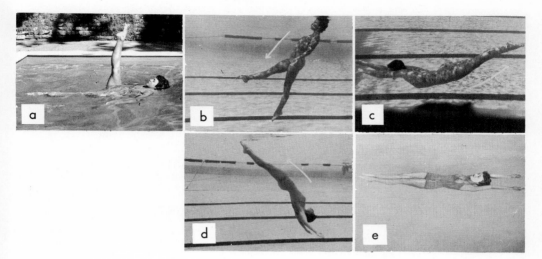

Plate 38

DOLPHIN, FOOT FIRST, BALLET LEG

Plate 38	*Starting Position*	*Measure*
a	Assume a right ballet leg position, hands near hips.	

Execution

	Hold the ballet leg position and start a foot first dolphin* by sculling at hips.	1-4
b	As the head submerges, bring the ballet leg toward the left leg. Use the same arm action as in a foot first dolphin.*	5-6
c, d	After the legs are brounght together, continue as in a foot first dolphin.*	7-10
e	Surface in a layout position on back.	11-12

Teaching Hints

At the time the head drops below the surface of the water, do not allow it to come forward or allow the body to pike, in order to get down. The small upward pulls of the arms at the sides of the shoulders should be sufficient.

See that the knees and ankles are fully extended throughout.

*Dolphin, Foot First, page 65.

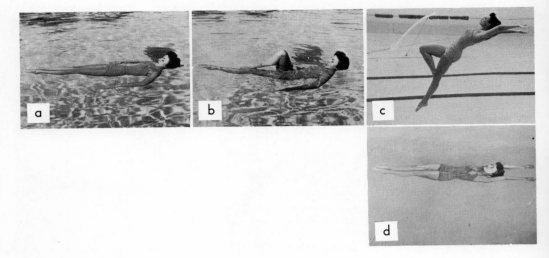

Plate 39

DOLPHIN, FOOT FIRST, BENT KNEE

Plate 39	*Starting Position*	*Measure*
a	Lie on back, body extended, hands near hips.	

Execution

b	Bring right knee toward the chest until the foot is beside the left knee.	1
c	Hold the bent knee position as the foot first dolphin* is being executed. Straighten the bent knee when it breaks the surface of the water as the dolphin circle is completed.	
d	Surface the body in a straight line, the same as in a dolphin*, foot first.	2-12

Teaching Hints

See that the right foot, with toes pointed, remains against the left knee. See that the left leg does not cut away from the path of the circle.

Watch the left foot as it surfaces, to see that the toes follow the surface of the water.

*Dolphin, Foot First, page 65.

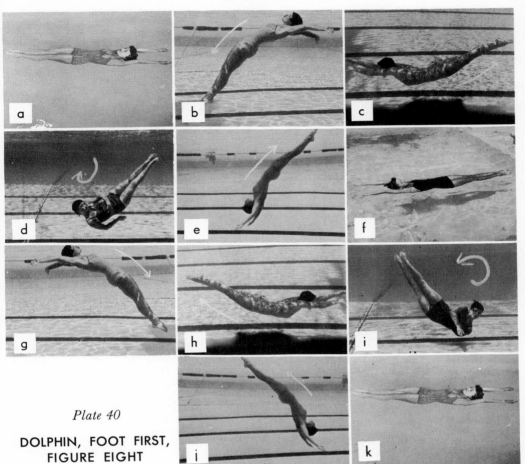

Plate 40

DOLPHIN, FOOT FIRST, FIGURE EIGHT

Plate 40	*Starting Position*	*Measure*
a	Lie on back, body extended, arms extended overhead.	

Execution

b, c	Start a foot first dolphin.	1-5
d	As the head passes the half-way point around the circle, execute a half roll.	6
e, f	Surface the body on the back, arms extended over the head facing in the opposite direction but in line with the starting position.	7, 8
g, h	Immediately start another foot first dolphin.*	9-13
i	As the body approaches the surface, execute a half roll.	14
j, k	Surface the body on the back in the original starting position.	15, 16

*Dolphin, Foot First, page 65.

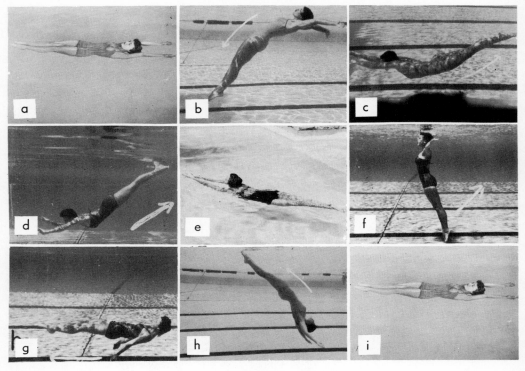

Plate 41

DOLPHIN, FOOT FIRST, FIGURE EIGHT VARIANT

Plate 41	*Starting Position*	*Measure*
a	Lie on back, body extended, arm overhead.	

Execution

b, c	Start a foot first dolphin.*	1-6
d	As the dolphin approaches the surface, straighten the body line and, by means of overhead sculling, return to the surface, feet first, in a layout position on the face.	7-9
e	Continue the movement toward the feet until the head emerges from the water. The feet remain close to the surface of the water during surfacing.	10-12
f	With legs extended, bring the feet downward to a point below the head, keeping the head above the water, body line straight. Now drop below the surface of the water.	13-16
g	Execute one complete circular arm pull, counterclockwise to bring the legs forward and start the movement in the direction of the feet. Correct any forward bend at the hips.	17-19

*Dolphin, Foot First, page 65.

h   Continue the movement toward the feet by sculling.   20-22

i   Return to the surface on the back. Resume the original
     starting position. (A figure eight has been described. Both
     halves of the figure eight should be the same size and shape.)   23, 24

Plate 42

DOLPHIN, FOOT FIRST, CHAIN

Plate 42   *Starting Position*   *Measure*

a   Two persons lie on back, one behind the other, connected
     by means of the feet at the neck. (In this illustration the
     girl is 1.)

Execution

The arms of participants pull in unison as the foot first
chain is started. 1 travels to a point below the starting position of the head of 2 before starting the upward progress.   1-8
                                                                    9-16
Return to the starting position.

Additional persons may be included in the chain.

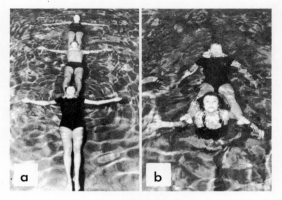

Plate 43

DOLPHIN, FOOT FIRST, PINWHEEL

Plate 43	*Starting Position*	*Measure*
a	Three persons lie on back, one behind the other, connected by means of the feet at the neck. (In this illustration, 1 is the girl at the bottom.)	

Execution

	Start as in a dolphin, foot first, chain.	1-8
b	1 makes a connection with head of 3 by means of the feet at neck, before 3 drops below the surface of the water. Complete one revolution of the wheel before the connection is broken at the same place.	9-16
	Return to starting position.	17-24

Additional persons may be added to the wheel.

Plate 44

DOLPHIN, CHAIN, MIXED

Plate 44	*Starting Position*	*Measure*
a	Two persons lie on back in a straight line, connected by the legs. (In this illustration, the boy is 1.)	

Execution

	1 executes a dolphin as 2 executes a foot first dolphin.	1-10

Additional persons may be added to the chain by connecting feet to necks.

Plate 45

DOLPHIN, FOOT FIRST, SUBMARINE

| Plate 45 | *Starting Position* | *Measure* |

a   Assume a right ballet leg position.

Execution

b, c   Hold ballet leg position and start a foot first dolphin* by sculling at hips.

The left leg is almost hyper-extended in following the path of the dolphin circle. Use the same arm action as in a foot first dolphin;* however, scull through the latter part of the execution.

Maintain stretch of the legs all the way around.

d   Continue until the left leg is horizontal on the surface of the water and ballet leg is at right angles to it and perpendicular to surface of water.   1-8

e   Lower the ballet leg (right) to the surface of the water to meet the left leg.   9-11

f   Finish in a back layout position.   12

Teaching Hints

See that knees and ankles are fully extended throughout the execution. Maintain a forceful backward press of left thigh during the execution.

Strive for height of ballet leg (right) above surface of water near close of stunt. Lower the leg with control so there is no splash.

See that left leg does not depress below the surface of water as right leg is being lowered.

*Dolphin, Foot First, page 65.

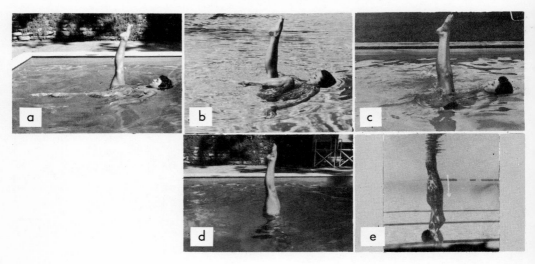

Plate 46

FLAMINGO

Plate 46	*Starting Position*	*Measure*
a	Execute a right ballet leg to the vertical position.	

Execution

b   Bring the left knee toward the chest, keeping the top of the left leg on the surface of the water. The left knee passes the right leg leaving the foot extended beyond the right leg (flamingo position).   1

c   Keeping the face above the surface of the water, extend the left leg to the vertical position of the right leg.   2

d   Hold the double ballet leg position. With no drop in the water level on the legs, roll the trunk backward onto the shoulders.

       The body assumes the vertical position. To roll the trunk backward, press downward with the arms. When they have pressed as far as possible, quickly rotate the arms outward at the shoulder joint and scoop the water to finish with the arms above the head.   3

e   Maintain balance and drop.   4

Teaching Hints

See that the double ballet legs do not lose elevation as the trunk rolls backward to put the body in a vertical position. A drop is due to the arms not working properly. The hands must press downward; arms must rotate outward at the shoulder joint with the finish above the head.

Achieve as much height as possible before dropping (Fig. 46d).

See that the trunk straightens first in the lower spine and follows through to the cervical area. Do not throw the head backward; this causes an arch in the back and a backward slant of the legs.

Keep the face above the surface of the water as the left leg assumes the vertical position.

Frequently the flexibility of the shoulder joint is limited. To increase flexibility, practice this exercise on the deck: Hold a towel three feet long, between the hands, in front of the face. Raise the arms straight and move the towel over the head behind the shoulders and return it to starting position, allowing no bend in elbows. Gradually shorten the width between hands.

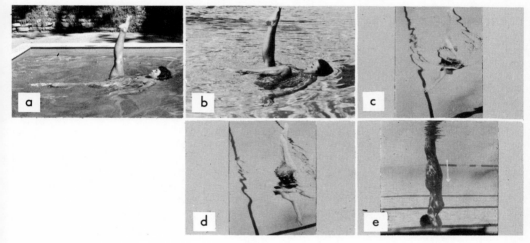

Plate 47

FLAMINGO, BENT KNEE

Plate 47	*Starting Position*	*Measure*
a	Assume a right ballet leg position.	

Execution

b	Bring left knee toward the chest (flamingo position).	1
c	Hold the above position and roll the trunk backward onto the shoulders to a vertical position before descending. The left foot is moved to the inside of the right leg. Achieve as much height as possible.	2
d	Maintain balance and extend left leg to meet the right leg before submergence of ankles.	3
e	Submerge (drop).	4

Plate 48

EIFFEL TOWER, AMERICAN

Plate 48	Starting Position	Measure
a	Assume extended right ballet leg position.	

Execution

b	Holding this ballet leg position, roll the body to the left.	1
c	Bring the head downward as the body pikes and ballet leg (right) moves across the surface of the water and meets the left leg.	2-3
d	Lift the left leg to the vertical.	4
e	Lift the right leg to meet the vertical left leg before the body submerges.	5
f	Submerge (drop).	6

Teaching Hints

See that the swimmer's right leg, with knee straight, remains on the surface of the water, as it travels across to meet the left leg.

The left leg should not depress as the right leg is moving across the surface of the water to meet it.

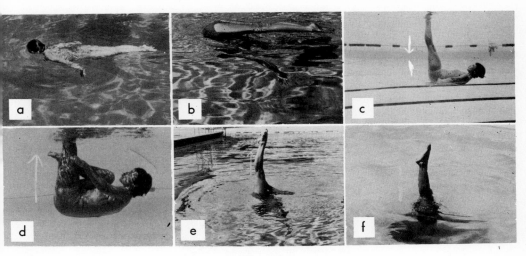

Plate 49

HERON

| Plate 49 | *Starting Position* | *Measure* |

a   Lie on face, body extended, hands near hips.

Execution

b, c   Execute a partial forward pike somersault* to the point at which the legs become vertical, with the water level between the knees and the ankles.   1-2

d   With no pause, bend right knee smoothly toward the chest (flamingo position) and raise the body toward the surface by sculling.

e   Just before the face reaches the surface, and with the water level below the left knee, drop the trunk to the vertical position, and at the same time thrust the left leg vertically out of the water. As the thrust is made, move the foot of the bent leg to the inside of the left leg. (To negotiate the drop of the trunk to the vertical and the thrust of the legs, press downward as far as possible with the arms, then rotate them outward at the shoulder joint and scoop the water until arms finish above the head.)   3-5

f   Submerge with the right leg still in bent knee position.   6

Teaching Hints

Maintain a sharp pike during the somersault.

For rotation of the body use the big circular arm movements described in the forward pike somersault.*

Keep the motion continuous during the entire execution of the stunt.

See that the back does not arch as the leg is thrust upward.

*Somersault, Forward Pike, page 92.

HERON SPINNING

The spin* of at least 180 degrees occurs at the height of the thrust.

Plate 50

KIP

Plate 50	*Starting Position*	*Measure*
a	Lie on back, body extended, hands near hips.	

Execution

b	Draw knees sharply toward chest.	1
c	Hold a tight tuck position and roll back onto the shoulders to an upside down, legs vertical, position. To bring the hips over the head, push downward with the hands. When they have pushed as far as they can go, quickly rotate the arms outward at the shoulder joint and scoop the water until the arms finish above the head.	2
d	Maintain balance, straighten the trunk, and extend the legs vertically upward before body descends in a vertical position. Achieve as much height as possible as the legs extend.	3
e	Submerge (drop).	4

Teaching Hints

See that a tight tuck is held.

Do not allow the head to drop backward as the legs extend, nor hips to move forward, causing back to arch. The unfolding starts in the lower spine and continues through the cervical area with the head coming into line last.

Maintain balance as legs are extended.

*Spins, page 96.

Plate 51

KIP, SPLIT

Plate 51		*Measure*

a   Separate the legs sideways or one leg forward and one back, just before the drop on the kip. Bring the legs together quickly, before submersion of the ankles. Keep the legs fully extended and tensed during the split.   4

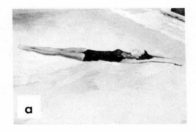

Plate 52

LOG ROLL

Plate 52	*Starting Position*	*Measure*

a   Lie on back or face, body extended, arms extended overhead.

Execution

Revolve the body to the right in a straight line by pressing down with the right shoulder.

Execute the roll close to the surface of the water. Stretch the body during execution.   1-2

Plate 53

MARCHING ON WATER

Plate 53	*Starting Position*	*Measure*
a	Lie on back, body extended.	

Execution

Bend left knee sharply and press against the water with back of calf and sole of foot. — 1

b — Reach forward gently with the left leg as the right knee is bent.

c — Continue, alternating legs. — 2

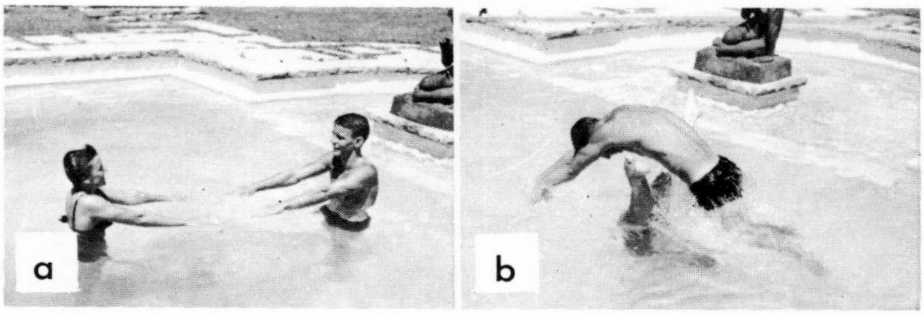

Plate 54

MONKEY ROLL

Plate 54	*Starting Position*	*Measure*
a	1 and 2 face each other, standing in shallow water. (In this illustration, 1 is the girl.)	

Execution

b — 1 executes a surface dive toward 2, spreading her feet apart. — 1, 2

2 dives through. Both turn to face each other. — 3,4

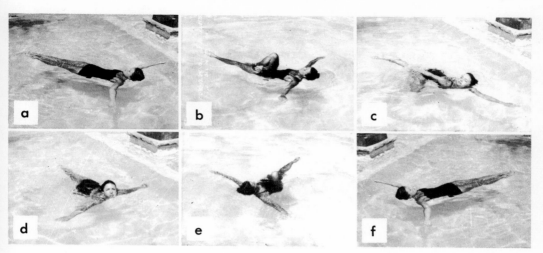

Plate 55

MARLIN

Plate 55	*Starting Position*	*Measure*

a   Lie on back, body extended, arms extended outward from shoulders.

Execution

b   Bring right knee toward chest.   1

c   Keeping the arms extended at 180 degree angle with each other during their rotation, and with the feet remaining in relatively the same spot, roll the body to the left by pressing back with the left shoulder and make a quarter twist. The right arm has cut through the water to the right hip; the left arm is directly opposite above the head. (Keep the feet close to the surface of the water, hands and arms under the surface of the water, and the body fully extended throughout. Do not scull.)   2

d   Continue rolling the body in the same direction for another quarter twist, to a face down position. Arms are fully extended outward from the shoulders.   3

e   Continue rolling in the same manner and in the same direction for two more quarter twists and finish on the back with arms fully extended outward from the shoulders.   4-5

f   Return bent knee to starting position. (The body is now at a right angle to its original starting position.)   6

The stunt may be executed in a bent knee position or with both legs straight. The face may be either in or out of the water.

Plate 56

MUSKRAT

Plate 56	*Starting Position*	*Measure*

Lie on face, body extended, legs together, back arched, hands close to hips.

Execution

a   Propel the body toward the head, on the surface by a sculling movement of the hands at the sides.   1-4

Submerge the body, retaining the same plane, by upward pressure of palms against the water. Continue the progress toward the head.   5-8

Return quietly to the surface, sculling forward on chest.   9-12

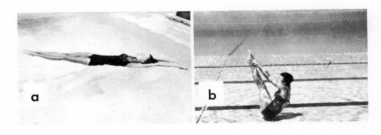

Plate 57

OYSTER

Plate 57	*Starting Position*	*Measure*

a   Lie on back, legs together, arms extended over head.

Execution

b   Bend sharply at hips and bring arms and hands out of water, over face to meet toes of extended legs. Fingers and toes meet directly above the hips.   1, 2

Hold position and drop below the surface of the water.   3,4

Plate 58

PENDULUM

Plate 58	*Starting Position*	*Measure*

a   Lie on back, body extended, arms overhead.

Execution

b   Swing the body downward in a straight line. Force the legs to sink by hyper-contraction of the abdominal muscles and the diaphragm (similar to sucking in the viscera). Contract the muscles of thighs and legs also. Exhale as much air as possible to assist with depressing the legs. Bring arms forward slowly to side horizontal position to help with balance.   1-8

c   After the body has passed beyond the perpendicular, take a breath. Allow head and arms to come forward. Hold the extended body position but gradually lessen the tension of the muscles as the body rises to the surface, face downward.   9-16

The pendulum may be reversed by starting on the face and ending in a float on the back.

Teaching Hints

Keep legs straight and together with no bend at hips or knees.
Hold the chin in normal position.
Allow no sculling.
The body movement from the head down resembles that of the pendulum of a clock.

Plate 59

PLANKS

Plate 59	*Starting Position*	*Measure*
a	Two persons float on back in tandem position. (1 is the girl in this illustration.)	

Execution

b	1 pulls the ankles of 2 and submerges, allowing 2 to glide over her until positions are reversed.	1-4
c	2 now pulls the ankles of 1 and submerges, allowing 1 to glide over him as both return to the original starting position.	5-8

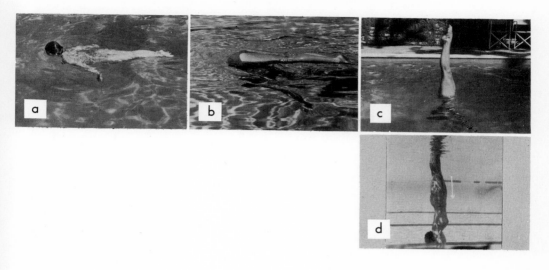

Plate 60

PORPOISE

Plate 60	*Starting Position*	*Measure*

a   Assume front layout position, arms extended near hips.

Execution

b   Keeping the legs close to the surface of the water, sweep the arms forward to pike the body.   1-2

c   Reverse the arm motion to a backward scoop as the legs are lifted to a position perpendicular to the surface of the water.   3

d   Submerge (drop).   4

Teaching Hints

Put the face in the water before starting the forward sweep of the arms.

Do not depress the legs and allow the buttocks to rise high out of the water when bending forward at the hips.

Do not pull the head too far under the hips.

Do not throw the head downward on the pike. Keep it in line with the trunk. Tighten abdominal muscles and pull trunk downward by sweep of the arms forward. Keep the arms close to the body on the forward sweep.

Do not allow the back to arch.

Plate 61

PORPOISE, FLYING

Plate 61	*Starting Position*	*Measure*

Stand in shallow water.

Execution

a	Bend knees, push off bottom of pool, and drive body vertically out of the water.	1, 2
b	Bend hips and bring head sharply downward.	3
c	Straighten the legs as the body enters the water head first.	4

Plate 62

PORPOISE, FLYING, DOUBLE

Plate 62	*Starting Position*	*Measure*

2 (the boy) stands on bottom of pool, knees bent, holding the feet of 1 in his hands.

Execution

a	2 throws 1, as 1 springs upward as much as possible.	1
	1 executes a porpoise at the top of the lift.	
b, c	2 immediately executes a flying porpoise.	2-4

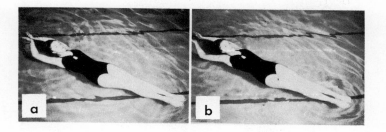

Plate 63

PROPELLER

Plate 63   *Starting Position*   *Measure*

Lie on back, body extended, arms over head.

Execution

a, b   Propel the body, feet first, by a sculling movement of the
hands overhead. Keep the face and tops of feet above surface
of water at all times.   1-8

Teaching Hints

Keep elbows close together during the sculling.

The hands execute a figure-eight sculling movement, not merely a backward push.

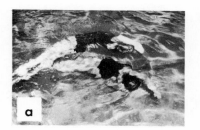

Plate 64

SHADOW STUNTING

A stunt is shadowed when two persons, one below the other, simultaneously
execute the same stunt.

Plate 64

a   Example of shark shadowed.

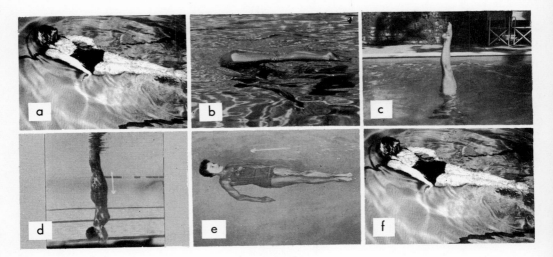

Plate 65

SEAL

Plate 65	*Starting Position*	*Measure*

a   Lie on face, head and heels out of the water, hands close to the hips.

Execution

b   Propel the trunk downward by sweeping the arms forward from the hips to pike the body.   1-2

c   Raise the legs over the head in a straight line with the body.   3

d   Submerge. Scull up head first on face.

e   Before surfacing, execute a half-roll of the body by sculling movements only and return to the surface head first, in a layout position on the back   4-5

f   Execute another half-roll immediately, on the surface of the water, to finish in the starting position.   6

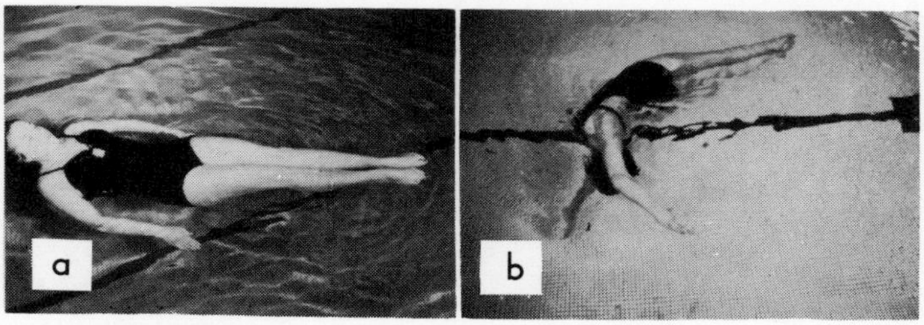

Plate 66

SHARK

Plate 66	*Starting Position*	*Measure*
a	Lie on back, body extended, hands at sides.	

Execution

b Turn on the left side with body just below and parallel to the surface of the water. Arch the body and extend right arm over the ear and parallel to the surface of the water, following the arc of the body. Keep the palm of the hand downward and just above the surface of the water.
Propel body part of the way around a circle by sculling with the left hand. Keep the knees straight and legs together, fully extended.

The position of the right arm may be varied.

SHARK CIRCLE

Execute a shark until a complete circle has been described.   8

SHARK FIGURE EIGHT

Complete one shark circle.   8

Turn to the opposite side with the opposite hand and arm over the head and complete another shark circle. (The two circles simulate a figure eight.)   8

Practice Hints

Walk on the bottom of the pool in three feet of water, assuming the body position of the shark. Walk through the movements, sculling with the lower arm.

Swim side stroke on the left side, bring right arm over the head, arch the back, and continue movement in the direction of the head.

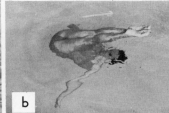

Plate 67

SOMERSAULT, BACK PIKE

| *Plate 67* | *Starting Position* | *Measure* |

a   Lie on back, legs together, body extended, hands near hips.

Execution

b   Keeping the legs close to the surface of the water, start the backward rotation of the body by bending sharply at the hips, legs straight, and pressing downward with the hands.

c   Holding pike position, continue pressing as far as possible with the hands and then quickly rotate the arms outward at the shoulder joints and continue scooping the water, to finish the rotation of the body. One complete circular movement of the arms rotating at the shoulder joint should be sufficient. Sculling may also be used to effect the rotation of the body. Hold the position and return to the surface, head upward.   1-4

d   Finish in a layout position on the back.

Teaching Hints

Execute the stunt close to the surface of the water.

Do not allow the buttocks to rise high above the surface of the water during the rotation.

Hold a tight pike throughout.

At the start of the stunt see that the body rotates without first dropping.

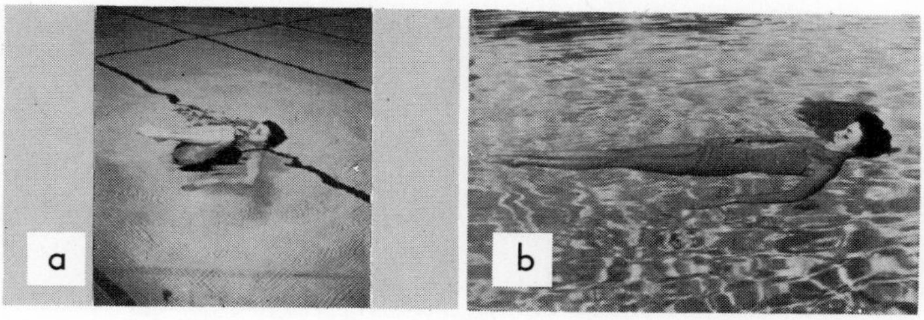

Plate 68

SOMERSAULT, BACK TUCK

Plate 68	*Starting Position*	*Measure*

a   Assume a tuck position.

Execution

The arm action in rotating the body in a back tuck somersault is similar to that used in a back pike somersault.* The head should remain tightly tucked until the body has made one complete rotation finishing with the head upward.

b   Finish in a layout position on the back.   1-4

---

*Somersault, Back Pike, p. 90.

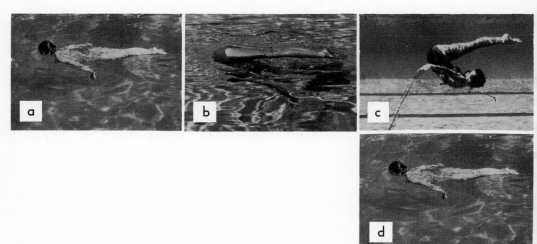

Plate 69

SOMERSAULT, FORWARD PIKE

| *Plate 69* | *Starting Position* | *Measure* |

a   Lie on surface of water, face downward, arms extended near hips.

Execution

b   Keeping the legs close to the surface of the water, sweep the arms forward as the body bends sharply at the hips.

c   Continue pressing upward with the arms as far as they will go and then quickly rotate the arms inward at the shoulder joint and continue pressing with the arms in the same big circular movement until the head returns to the surface.   1-4

d   Finish in a layout position on the face.

Sculling may also be used to rotate the body.

Practice Hints

Execute the stunt just below the surface of the water.

Do not allow the buttocks to rise high above the suface of the water.

Do not allow legs to depress as the body bends forward. Place the face in the water before starting either arm or body action.

Plate 70

SOMERSAULT, FORWARD TUCK

Plate 70	*Starting Position*	*Measure*

a   Assume back layout position, arms extended near hips.

Execution

b   Draw knees toward chest and tuck head tightly. Rotate the body forward using the same arm action as that used in the forward pike somersault.* The head should remain tucked until the body has made one complete revolution, head upward.

c   Finish in back layout position.   1-4

Sculling movements may also be used to rotate the body.

Teaching Hints

Execute the stunt close to the surface of the water.
Do not allow the buttocks to rise high above the water level.

---

*Somersault, Forward Pike, p. 92.

Plate 71

SOMERSAULTS, TANDEM

| *Plate 71* | *Starting Position* | *Measure* |

Bodies in vertical position, partners' hands joined, arms extended at sides, face to face.

Execution

a   Pull on hands and draw knees to chest.   1

Roll simultaneously forward. Hold position, continue around, and return to surface.   2-4

The tandems may be back to back as well as face to face.

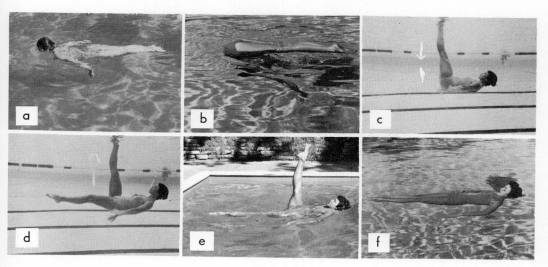

Plate 72

SOMER-SUB

Plate 72	*Starting Position*	*Measure*
a	Lie on face, body extended, legs together, hands near hips.	

Execution

b	Start a forward pike somersault.*	1-2
c	Continue around until the legs are vertical, trunk horizontal.	3-4
d	Drop one leg to the horizontal position, parallel to the surface of the water.	5
e	Hold position and surface.	6-7
f	Finish in a layout position on back.	8

Teaching Hints

See that the horizontal leg does not float up. It should remain horizontal after it has dropped.

See that the legs do not separate before they have reached the vertical position.

Allow no bend at the knees.

*Somersault, Forward Pike, page 92.

Plate 73

SPINS

Plate 73	*Starting Position*	*Measure*

a   Vertical, head downward, legs as high as possible above the water, arms extended beyond the head.

Execution

The spin is used on stunts in which the legs have been thrust high out of the water. The spin occurs at the top of the thrust.

b   Execute a fast turn of the body at least 180 degrees to the right in one quick movement, by employing a forceful turn of the arms and shoulders. Whip left arm across in front of the face and the right arm toward the back of the head. As soon as the left arm whips across in front of the face, push it back to the left against the water to help with the spin. Hold the right arm for balance and scull with the right hand to keep the body high.   1

c   Submerge (drop).   2

Spins may be added to stunts in which the body is in an upside-down vertical position and in which there is sufficient lift or thrust. The following are examples: the barracuda group and the heron.

Plate 74

SPIRAL

Plate 74	*Starting Position*	*Measure*
a	Vertical, head downward.	

Execution

| a | Execute four full twists* in the starting position. | |
| | Submerge (drop). | 1-16 |

*Twists, page 104.

Plate 75

SUBMARINE, SINGLE BALLET LEG

Plate 75	*Starting Position*	*Measure*
a	Lie on back, body extended, legs together, hands close to hips.	

Execution

b	Draw right knee toward chest until thigh is perpendicular to the surface of water.	1
c	Extend right leg to the vertical position with no movement of knee toward chest. Height of ballet leg above water is desirable.	2
d	Holding this position, submerge the body until the ankle of the ballet leg is at water level.	3-4
e	Rise to the suface by sculling, holding the right ballet leg position, until the face is out of the water.	5-6
f	Bend knee with no movement of knee toward chest.	7
g	Resume original starting position.	8

Traveling may occur at any time during the execution of the stunt.

Practice Hints

Do not allow horizontal left leg to float up while under water. It should remain horizontal.

Do not return right leg to bent knee position before face has surfaced.

Plate 76

SUBMARINE, DOUBLE BALLET LEGS

Plate 76	*Starting Position*	*Measure*
a	Lie on back, body extended, hands close to hips.	

Execution

b	Draw both knees toward the chest until thighs are perpendicular to surface of water.	1
c	Extend legs simutaneously to double ballet leg position, with no movement of knees toward chest. Height of legs above water is desirable. Face must remain above surface of the water.	2
d	Holding this position, submerge body until the ankles are at water level.	3-4
e	Rise to the surface by sculling, holding the vertical double ballet leg position until the face is out of the water.	5-6
f	Bend knees with no movement of knees toward chest.	7
g	Resume original starting position.	8

Traveling may occur at any time during execution of the stunt.

Teaching Hints

See that the hips are not too low in water on the double ballet legs.

See that legs are not leaning toward head; they should be perpendicular to surface of water.

See that knees in the extended ballet leg position are not bent.

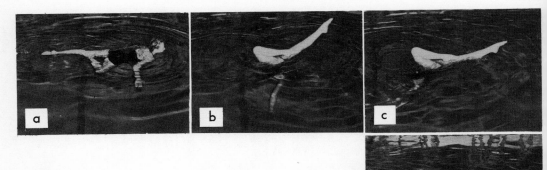

Plate 77

SWORDFISH

Plate 77	*Starting Position*	*Measure*

a   Lie on face, one knee bent, head and heel of extended leg above surface of water, hands near hips.

Execution

b, c   Submerge the head and extend the leg out of the water until the body is over-balanced onto the back. This is accomplished by pressing forward with the hands as far as they will go and then quickly rotating the arms inward at the shoulder joints, continuing with the pressure through one complete circular arm movement and finishing above the head. Continue movement on back toward feet. Straighten the bent knee as it breaks the surface of the water.   1-5

d   Finish in a layout position on back as in a foot first dolphin.   6

Teaching Hints

Allow no upward lunge of head and shoulders before their submersion. See that arms are straight during the pull.

The hands start their forward presure from the hips immediately. If the arms press forward, not out to the side as they press toward the head, the arm action will be more effective.

See that the leg does not travel in jerks over the water. This is due to short ineffective arm pulls instead of a big circular pull with inward rotation at the shoulder joint.

See that the hips do not drop low in the water. This is due to a discontinuance of the hand and arm action.

Plate 78

TAILSPIN

Plate 78	*Starting Position*	*Measure*

a   Lie on left side in shark* position.

Execution

a, b   Propel the body as in a shark.* Describe at least three revolutions while maintaining a uniform continuous change of body angle until the body is in a vertical position, head downward with feet at water level. Momentum is obtained by sculling. The change of body plane is accomplished by lowering the head slightly and by sculling the body downward.   1-13

c   Before submerging, execute one-half twist† in a vertical   14-15
position, head downward with feet at water level.

Submerge (drop).   16

*Shark, p. 89.
†Twists, p. 104.

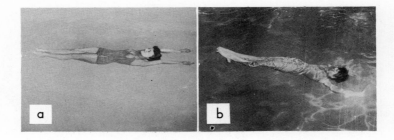

Plate 79

TORPEDO

Plate 79	*Starting Position*	*Measure*

a   Lie on back, body fully extended, arms over head.

Execution

Scull toward the feet.

b   With an upward push of the hands against the water, submerge the head and shoulders. Feet and ankles remain on surface of the water.

Continue sculling.

Return to the surface in starting position.   1-8

Teaching Hints

Keep elbows close together, slightly beyond shoulder width.

The hands execute a figure eight sculling movement, not merely a backward push.

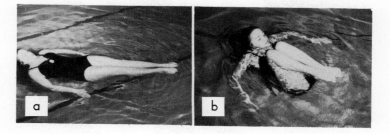

Plate 80

TUB

| *Plate 80* | *Starting Position* | *Measure* |

a Lie on back, body extended, hands near hips.

Execution

b Draw knees to chest, keeping feet and legs together, toes   1
pointed and on the surface of the water. The body rests
further back than the sitting position. Hold a tight tuck
and spin the body in a circle using an opposite sculling
motion of the hands; one hand presses the water toward
the feet; the other hand presses the water away from the
feet.   2-8

Plate 81

TWISTS

Plate 81   *Starting Position*   *Measure*

Vertical, head downward, arms almost straight, hands in
front of the face. Legs remain out of the water at an optional
level between the knees and ankles.

Execution

a   Execute a half twist (180 degrees) to the right. Scull with
the left hand to gain leverage and balance. Scull with the
right hand to gain leverage, balance, and to negotiate the
twist.   1-4

Execute a full twist (360 degrees) in the same manner.

Practice Hints

See that the body revolves on its central axis.
Maintain a stationary level of the legs in the water.
Avoid traveling.
Keep the hips in line with the trunk.
Avoid excessive arch in the back.
Twists may be added to many stunts. The following are examples: kip,
porpoise, flamingo, catalina, dolphin, and dolphin, foot first.

Plate 82

WALKING ON HANDS IN DEEP WATER (PERISCOPE)

Plate 82	*Starting Position*	*Measure*
a	Lie on face, body extended, legs together.	

Execution

b Execute a porpoise* to a depth at which the legs remain out of the water to about mid-calf. Arms are extended overhead. Scull to maintain water level at near mid-calf. 1-2

c Maintain balance as the body is propelled toward the heels by a sculling action of the hands. Travel a distance of several feet. 3-8

Plate 83

WALKOVER, BACK

Plate 83	*Starting Position*	*Measure*
	Lie on back, body extended, hands near hips.	

Execution

a, b Start a dolphin†. Raise the right leg and continue its movement in an arc over the surface of the water. As it reaches the surface, life the left leg and continue its movement in an arc over the surface until it meets the right leg. 1-4

c The body surfaces in a front layout position with movement toward the feet. 5-6

*Porpoise, page 85.
†Dolphin, page 57.

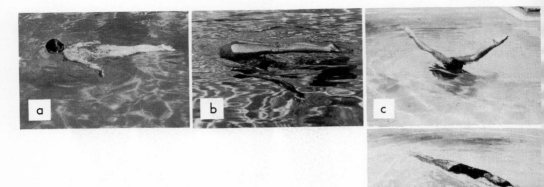

Plate 84

WALKOVER, FRONT

Plate 84	*Starting Position*	*Measure*
a	Lie on face, body extended, hands near hips.	

Execution

b	Draw body into a sharp pike position.	1
c	Scull to maintain body height while raising the left leg and bringing it in an arc over the surface of the water as the back arches. When the left leg reaches the water, bring the right leg over in its arc. The legs meet on the surface of the water.	2-3
d	Finish on the back in a layout position.	4

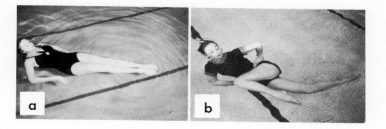

Plate 85

WATER WHEEL

Plate 85	*Starting Position*	*Measure*
a	Lie on back, body extended, hands near hips.	

Execution

b   Turn on side, hands on hips, bring knee toward chest. Turn head slightly until the face is out of the water.   1

Execute a pedaling movement of the legs to move the body in a circle with the head and shoulders as a pivot. Keep the legs close to the surface of the water.   2-7

Return to the starting position.   8

The position of the hands is optional as long as they do not aid in propelling the body.

6

PATTERNS

In synchronizing water techniques the swimmer, as a member of a team, must adapt his skills to the requirements of the group. He must continually be aware of his position in a pattern, using definite pool markings if they are helpful, and he must anticipate the next pattern, keeping the signals for changing in mind. In floating patterns he must be able to float and scull very easily and to maintain contact lightly but firmly with the adjoining floaters. Concentration is of the utmost importance.

The movement from one pattern to another may be indicated in various ways. Until the swimmers learn the patterns, the teacher may indicate the time to change by admonitions or percussive means. When the routine is finished, one of the leaders or the key swimmers who are strategically placed in the pattern may indicate the moment to change. They signal by nodding or lifting the hand slightly. All swimmers start moving on the next measure. If each swimmer can synchronize with the music independently of the others, the phrases of the music are good indicators for changes.

After the swimmers have performed and timed the routine in the water, land practice is helpful. Synchronizing the stroke and stunt movements outside of the water to the accompanying music or to a rhythmic counting not only reviews the succession of skills but also emphasizes their proper timing.

In the patterns presented on the following pages, sequences are suggested for many. Where stunts are involved, others than those named may be substituted. In two cases the patterns may be described in shallow water by good beginners, substituting the very simplest skills. The variations of the standard strokes pictured in Chapter 4 add to the effectiveness of the patterns. Remember that a stroke means two complete arm pulls in the crawls and the glide in the other strokes.

JOINED LINES IN MOTION

Have the swimmers in contact, forming one continuous line—horizontal, vertical, or curving—or forming a raft (a combination of horizontal and vertical lines). Their free arms and legs propel the line. First, teach two swimmers to float on their backs, joining at the shoulder with the hand when side by side, and under the arms or at the neck with the feet when in a vertical line. Next, teach them to scull the length of the pool with the free arm and to back crawl kick with the free legs. Each swimmer must learn to think of his position in relation to the others. Emphasize keeping the legs and arms straight all the time. After this preliminary practice, increase the number of swimmers in a line.

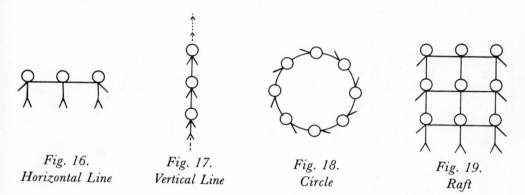

Fig. 16.	Fig. 17.	Fig. 18.	Fig. 19.
Horizontal Line	*Vertical Line*	*Circle*	*Raft*

Practice the following lines in motion:

A horizontal line (Fig. 16) of any number of swimmers

When on the side, hold the upper shoulder of the next swimmer with the hand of the top arm; propel with the lower arm and synchronize scissors kick.

When on the back, hold shoulders with hands; all kick in unison, and the two end swimmers use their outside arms.

A vertical (Fig. 17) or curving line of any number

When on the side, hold the hand of the swimmers ahead and behind; synchronize scissors kick.

When on the back, attach feet lightly under the arms or to the neck of the next swimmer and propel with arms.

A circle of eight (Fig. 18) or more

When on the side, hold hands as in Fig. 17 and synchronize scissors kick.

When on the back, attach feet lightly under the arms or to the neck of the swimmer in front; propel in unison with outside arm.

A raft (Fig. 19)

When on the back, propel in unison with the outside arms; the last line kicks.

WEAVING PATTERNS

Weaving patterns have a quality of producing suspense which is excellent for maintaining interest.

Parallel zigzags (Fig. 20)

6, 5, and 4 swim to line *A* and tread water. 1, 2, and 3 time their strokes with 6, 5, and 4 as they pass and swim with them to line *A* and on to line *B* and tread water. Then 6, 5, and 4 swim to line *C* and tread, picking up 1, 2, and 3 at *B*. 1, 2, and 3 continue to line *D* and tread. Continue.

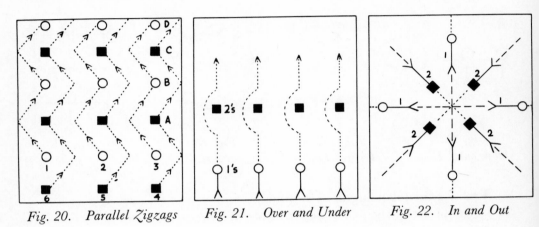

Fig. 20.   *Parallel Zigzags*   Fig. 21.   *Over and Under*   Fig. 22.   *In and Out*

Over and under (Fig. 21)

1's porpoise dive under or leap frog over 2's. Continue.

In and Out (Fig. 22)

Advanced—2's swim to center as 1's swim out; change. 2's do stunts as 1's swim out and in.

Beginners in shallow water—substitute glides, kicking and churn stunts.

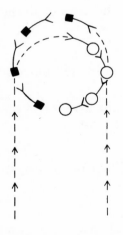

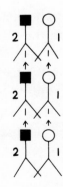

Fig. 23.   *Forming a Circle*   Fig. 24.   *Legs Cross*

Forming a circle (Fig. 23)

Make a circle from two lines, using an even number of swimmers.

Legs cross (Fig. 24)

2's swim regular side stroke; 1's use reverse kick.

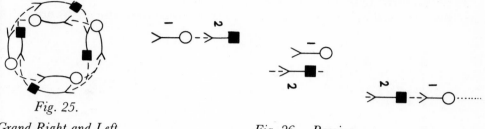

Fig. 25.

Grand Right and Left   *Fig. 26.   Passing*

In a circle or figure eight pattern pass right and left shoulders.

Passing (Fig. 26)

1 follows 2 for two strokes; 1 passes 2 in two strokes; 2 follows 1 for two strokes; continue. This passing may be done when swimming in a circle, line, figure eight, or zigzag course.

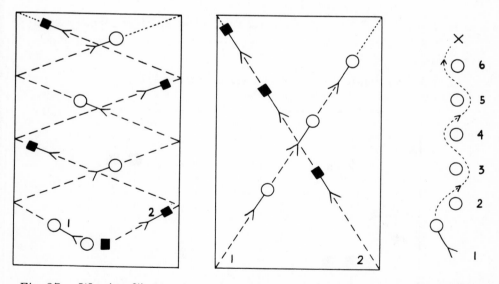

Fig. 27.   Weaving Zigzags   *Fig. 28.   Diagonal Crossing Fig. 29. Weaving Line*

Weaving zigzags (Fig. 27) and diagonal crossing (Fig. 28)

1 starts one stroke after the first swimmer; each succeeding swimmer starts one stroke after the preceding.

Weaving vertical line (Fig. 29)

1 swims along the dotted line and stops at *X;* 2 follows two strokes later, followed in turn by the others.

PATTERNS WITH AN ACCENT

These patterns may serve as accents in a routine. They also produce suspense since the swimmers come so close together that they appear to bump.

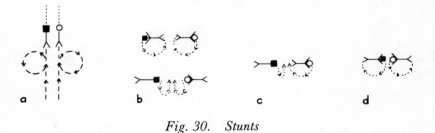

Fig. 30.   Stunts

Stunts (Fig. 30)

Two swimmers or two lines of swimmers start or finish stunts close together, sometimes starting and finishing with hands touching.

    a. The hand in the air in the shark stunt just misses or touches that of partner as each completes the circle.

    b. Both do dolphins or porpoises and come up close together.

    c. 1 does a fast dolphin, 2 does a porpoise, and both come up close together.

    d. Both do dolphins going down very close together.

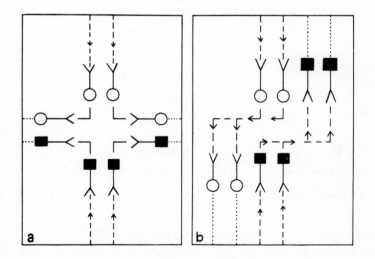

Fig. 31.   Forward and Turn

Forward and turn (Fig. 31)

Couples swim in unison toward each other. At the moment that they expect to meet

a. Those on the right turn right; those on the left turn left.
b. Couples turn to the right, swim one stroke, turn to the left and swim.

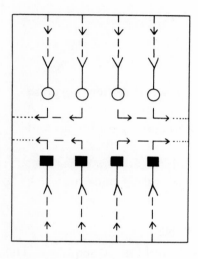

Fig. 32.   Head On

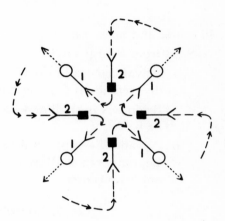

Fig. 33.   To Center and Turn

Head on (Fig. 32)

Lines swim in unison toward each other. At the moment that they expect to meet

the lines make right and left angle turns, or

the lines reverse turn and retrace paths, or

the lines porpoise dive or forward somersault and come up facing (dolphin or back somersault if swimming on back), or

one line, if swimming crawl or breast stroke, porpoise dives under the other.

To center and turn (Fig. 33)

All swim toward center like wheel spokes. 1's are one stroke ahead of 2's. 1's make sharp turns to the right at the moment that they expect to meet in the center; 2's do the same thing when they reach center.

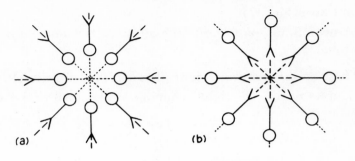

Fig. 34.   To Center and Back

To center and back (Fig. 34)

Start from a large circle.

a. Advanced—all crawl or breast stroke toward center, porpoise dive, come up holding hands.

Beginners in shallow water—face glide to center, double up and lie back.

b. Advanced—scull out from center and dolphin.

Beginners in shallow water—gently push off on back and kick out from center.

SEQUENCES OF PATTERNS

Many patterns follow each other in a smooth and logical sequence. The sequences presented here are based on the accordion, circle, and wheel patterns.

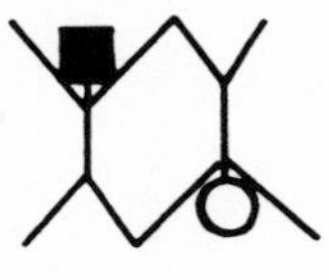

Fig. 35.   Floating Duet

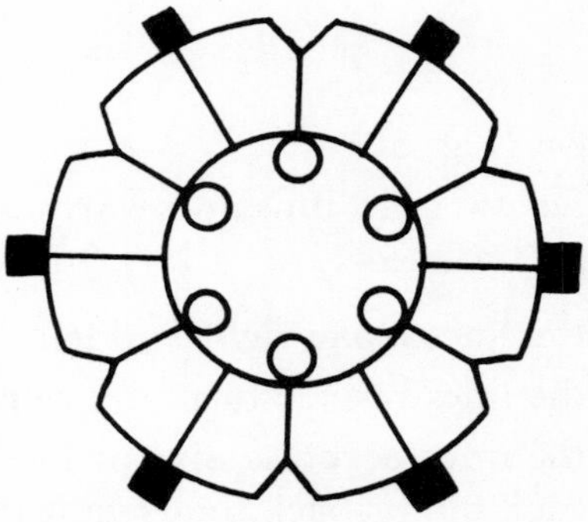

Fig. 36.   In a Circle

ACCORDIONS

Floating duet (Fig. 35)

Practice floating in pairs. Both swimmers float on their backs, side by side, facing in opposite directions with arms and legs spread. With the inside hand, grasp lightly under the ankle of partner. Keep legs and arms straight. Revolve by synchronizing sculling or elementary back arm pull with the outside arm.

In a circle (Fig. 36)

For twelve: The center six with arms straight hold the elbow of the adjacent floater; the outer six with arms straight hold their feet, and float with their own feet together and touching lower arms of the inside six. Before the outer six float, they may scissors kick the circle around once.

For ten: Use similar technique.

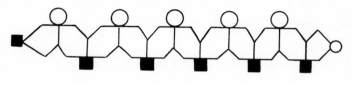

Fig. 37.   In a Line

In a line (Fig. 37)

Make a line accordion from the preceding circular one. Break the circle at one point. Each of the two end swimmers takes hold of the hand and ankle of the one next to him while each of the remaining inside floaters take hold of the ankles of the outside five floaters. The two end swimmers scissors kick the floating circle slowly and steadily into a long accordion.

Close and open the accordion. The two end swimmers, using scissors kick, close it from the ends, the floaters in succession closing legs and bringing arms to the side. The two end swimmers open the accordion in reverse manner.

The accordion may also be closed and opened from one end only.

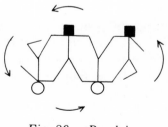

Fig. 38.   Revolving

Revolving (Fig. 38)

Form three small accordions of four floaters from the long line of twelve —the two end swimmers of the line of twelve join the line of floaters and the line breaks between the fourth and fifth and the eighth and ninth floaters. The outside floaters of the three small groups put outside foot on the knee and, using a sculling motion, revolve each accordion once. Connect the three small ones back into the long line accordion again. All release grasp. Splash back crawl kick in two lines to the sides of the pool.

CIRCLES. The following patterns are effective when the side and side overarm strokes, standard or modified as pictured in Chapter 4, are swum throughout; or when the side and side overarm strokes, standard or modified, are swum on the straight lines and the shark stunt describes the circular patterns; or when either the front or back crawl stroke is swum on the straight lines and the shark stunt describes the circular patterns.

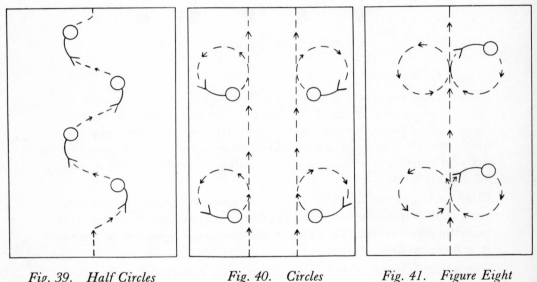

Fig. 39. Half Circles   Fig. 40.   Circles   Fig. 41.   Figure Eight

Half circles (Fig. 39)

Swim one stroke straight up the pool, and start describing a wavy line by swimming half circles on alternate sides of the center line, always with the back to the line. Roll onto the other side as the center line is crossed. As one swimmer follows another or as one parallels another, they synchronize their positions and skills.

Circles (Fig. 40)

Two swimmers take two strokes up the pool. Each describes a small circle, six feet in diameter, with the back to the center of the circle. They swim two more strokes up the pool and repeat the small circles. Other couples follow and synchronize their strokes and positions with those preceding them.

Figure eight (Fig. 41)

Swim two strokes up the pool and describe a circle as suggested in Fig. 40. Immediately roll onto the other side and describe a similar circle on the other side of the center line, the two circles forming a figure eight. Swim two strokes up the pool and repeat. Others following synchronize their positions and skills.

Variation: Two swimmers in single file take two strokes up the pool. 1 does a shark figure eight, starting to the right; 2 takes one more arm pull and does a shark figure eight starting to the left. 1 crosses the center line in the middle of the figure eight just ahead. 2 completes the shark eight just after 1 and synchronizes his crawl stroke with 1 as they continue in single file up the pool to repeat the figure eight.

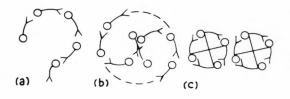

(a)   (b)   (c)

Fig. 42.   Spoked Wheel

Wheels

The spoked wheel (Fig. 42)

a. Eight swimmers stroke on the right side up the center of the pool and form one large circle.

b. On signal they swim into two small circles of four each.

c. They swim around once in the two small circles holding left hands in the center with elbows straight and then swim back into the large circle.

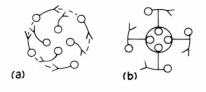

(a)   (b)

Fig. 43.   Floating Wheel

The floating wheel (Fig. 43)

a. Advanced—eight swimmers stroke on the right side in one large circle. On signal every other one swims into the center.

Beginners in shallow water—substitute the dog paddle for the side stroke.

b. Advanced—the inner four roll onto the back and float while holding the shoulders of the adjacent floaters. The outer four take hold
of the feet of the inner four with the left hand, pull them out and
swim the floaters around once, using scissors kick and right arm
pull. This pattern may be followed with one in which the four inner
ones porpoise dive under the four outer ones, and then with the
pattern described in Fig. 33.

Beginners in shallow water—the inner four float; the outer four
take hold of the feet of the floaters and move them around once.
Follow this pattern with the circular pattern for beginners in Fig. 22.

7

WATER COMPOSITION

The impulse to express an idea through swimming starts the development of a water composition. The inspiration for the idea may come from a particular melody or rhythm that moves one kinesthetically, or the character of a piece of music may arouse a mood that seeks expression. The impulse may originate in a flair for comedy, for drama, or for parody, or in a desire to mold outstanding swimming ability into an expressive unit.

The idea is the motivation; it gives purpose and acts as a unifying thread throughout the composition. Without a purpose the result is just an arrangement of techniques or designs that lack a center of attention. An idea gives a point of interest for the audience; they appreciate a number in the proportion in which they are able to react to it. The character and mood.of the idea give the composition substance and meaning.

MUSIC

The music used in synchronized swimming is equally important because a good swimming composition is one in which the swimming movements and their designs identify themselves so well with the music that the result is a unit. The music does not dominate; it guides and inspires, leaving the attention focused on the swimming. It is best if the development of the idea and the choice of the music can evolve together, at the same time giving consideration to the ability of the swimmers. If suitable music cannot be found promptly, it is wise to formulate the idea only roughly until the music is located. It may save many hours of searching and necessary changes in prearranged plans. The music is fundamentally important because once decided upon, it establishes the mood and character of the swimming—of course, the mood and character of the music determined its choice originally—and its structural form guides the designing.

At this point musical analysis is necessary: to reiterate—recognize the theme, its recurrence and variations, contrasting music, climax, introduction, coda or end, and determine the over-all form, such as *A B A*. Suggestions are made in Chapter 2 for musical analysis, and actual notation of all these points is necessary in order to have a clear picture of the musical structure, the proportion of each part to the whole, and the general feeling of the music. Listen attentively to the music until you can anticipate what comes next. Literally it should become a part of you. This close identification with the music helps to create a swimming choreography that flows with the music.

CHOREOGRAPHY

Though the musical form is a guide in the structure of the water choreography, it does not mean that every swimming phrase must literally follow every musical phrase as it repeats and varies. The swimming choreography is a creative thing in itself. The length of each part and of the whole water composition is determined by that of the music, and within these boundaries the choreographer expresses the character of the music as he blends the aquatic movement with the music. Just how the idea is expressed in the water and how a unified and interesting development of the idea is designed depends upon the choreographer's concept of the idea and his response to the music. With experience it will increase in subtlety and originality of expression.

He chooses the swimming skills, movements, and gestures according to the ability of his group. He realizes how these skills may be modified and combined, how space, level, direction, and focus all play a part in the use of a skill to develop the idea. Simple gestures and movements can be very effective and meaningful. It is the way they are done and the way they are synchronized with each other and with the music rather than the difficulty that appeals. Many observers do not realize what is difficult but they do respond to expression in the swimming. They are impressed, for instance, by strong, dynamic movements where the music increases in volume and tempo, by smoothly flowing stunts and strokes to lyrical rhythms, by good timing and feeling for syncopation in syncopated music, by the focus of movements toward a definite point, by sharp movements on staccato notes, by good synchronization of the skills.

No one can tell a person how to create. There is no set pattern. There are underlying principles that guide the creation of all art forms whether they be painting, writing, music, or water composition. They are unity, variety, contrast, and climax, and consciously or subconsciously artists are aware of these flexible guides.

Unity. Unity is the most fundamental principle in any type of composition. The idea which is identified with, or closely tied to, the music is the co-ordinating factor; it permeates and is evident throughout the water composition. If the idea is the expression of a certain mood, unity may be gained through the selection of those water skills that in the mind of the choreographer best convey that feeling. If the idea came from a dance rhythm, water movements that point up the particular rhythmic concept tend to unify the composition. Concretely, the expression of the idea starts with an aquatic movement that suggests the idea and acts as a springboard. It should be sufficiently interesting and adaptable so that it can be repeated and varied and, with the introduction of contrasting skills, be developed to a high point of interest, the climax. Sometimes a single skill, a stunt, or a stroke is an adequate basis upon which to build an idea, and again a different idea might call for a more complex movement, such as a four-measure phrase of two front crawl arm pulls and a turn on the last two measures. A method of discovering an appropriate aquatic movement or theme is to experiment in the water to the mood and rhythm of the theme music; one of the improvisations will be effective to a critical observer and can be molded into a clear-cut aquatic theme movement. It may take two, four, or eight measures of music. It is simply stated at first to allow for an increase in action and interest as the designing proceeds.

Planning successively each of the parts, *A B A*, seeking variety and unity within each part and in proportion to the total idea, is good procedure. It gives a sense of unity within each part and produces a feeling of repose in the large plan as the phrasing of measures does within the parts. The short forms of composition are helpful in designing the parts.

REPETITION. In general, in developing the aquatic movement it is well to repeat it, because repetition emphasizes the idea and establishes a familiarity with it and produces a feeling of harmony and agreement. This is also true when the aquatic movement is repeated or recalled in the second *A* part or in the coda at the end.

VARIETY. Continual repetition makes for monotony, so a variation of the aquatic movement is necessary. The development that follows and impels the idea forward grows out of the aquatic movement or relates to it or points it up. The number and ability of the swimmers help to determine the selection of skills and patterns used to do this. The music in conjunction with the idea is a guide as to when to use them. Ways to achieve variety are: (1) Introduce more swimmers—for example, the first two swim an aquatic movement in four measures and continue, the second two start the movement when the first couple repeat it, the third two start on the next repetition. (2) Introduce related skills—the back and front crawl strokes complement each other as do the side and single overarm strokes, the breast and elementary backstrokes, and front and back somersaults. (3) Change the line of direction—all swimmers swim an aquatic movement and, on a repetition of it later, the group swims in a different direction or a part of the group only changes direction. This can lead to various pattern changes. (4) Change the tempo—change from the regular tempo of the crawl to one twice as fast, as may be done in a tango movement; or, conversely, change to one one-half as fast as the regular tempo, as may be done in a march. (5) Change the level—the stunt submarine offers a variation in level to the ballet leg stunt. (6) Modify a technique—in doing a stunt or stroke, vary a hand, arm, leg, or head movement; add a turn or swing of the body, of the leg, or of the arm. (7) Repeat the first part of an aquatic movement but vary the second part—vary the phrase, three slow crawl arm pulls and two fast ones, by spiraling on the two fast ones.

CONTRAST. As the idea develops, a contrast in movement is welcomed in the large plan and possibly within each part. Within the designing of each part the introduction of a contrasting skill in the form of a stunt, a stroke, a turn, or a sustained movement, for example, and one that follows logically in the development is effective; as, also, is contrast in parallel movement or tempo— that is, one group swims the front crawl stroke while another swims the back crawl, or one group swims the crawl half as fast as another group, or part of a group swims around the others who are making a floating pattern, or the swimmers effect a sustained movement during fast music.

In the large *A B A* form, B is the contrasting part in which the mood or rhythm is different from that of *A*. Therefore, in the *B* part another aquatic theme or movement is introduced. In whatever form it takes it is different from the aquatic theme of *A* and yet related in some way so that it results in enhancing the development of the movement in *A*. Swimming offers endless contrasting materials that harmonize with different ideas and music. Strokes and their many variations synchronize with any rhythmic scheme. The numerous stunts express all moods and tempos and add new interest with their underwater movements. Floating patterns of both a stationary and moving type and interchanging patterns provide special interest on both the vertical and horizontal planes. Swimming a slow crawl to Chopin's "Minute Waltz" is an example of effective contrast in swimming and musical tempos.

TRANSITION. In any part of the composition, unless the idea suggests otherwise, the change from one skill to another—such as stroke to stunt, stroke to stroke, stunt to stunt or pattern—should not be marked by a stop in movement. When a change is to be made, the end of one skill should place the swimmer in position to start the next one. For example, in changing from back crawl stroke to a dolphin stunt: stroke right, left, right; leave the left arm in back of the head until the right arm recovers, and then continue into the back dolphin. Then the transition will be smooth, the action continuous, and the attention carried along in the development of the idea.

The few transitional measures that are sometimes between parts of the music are separate little entities used by the choreographer to connect the swimming movements of the larger and separate parts. They unobtrusively but purposefully lead one on to the different mood, rhythm, or tempo of the part to follow. It is important in all transitions that there be no "dead spots"— that is, moments of inactivity when obviously waiting for a particular measure or note. Practically any swimming skill can be used for transitions as long as it has meaning in the design and harmonizes with the music. A stunt that ends one part of the composition does not have to be completed in the standard way; it can be modified to permit swimming under water to a position for the following part. Emerging from the water may be done quietly or forcefully, followed by a skill that introduces the mood of the next part. If there are no transitional measures in the music, the choreographer can design the end of each part (if necessary, he can modify the final skill) in such a way that the swimmers are in position for swimming the following part.

CLIMAX. The major climax is the high spot of the composition. The aquatic idea is developed in a significant way to a culminating point. The climax of the swimming choreography synchronizes with that of the music. The manner of expressing the climax is important so that all the choreographic material can build toward it. The climax in swimming may be achieved through an increase in the tempo of the swimming, and/or in the sounds made by the swimmers, by a concentration of all the swimmers toward the same spot, by a feeling of repose after vigorous swimming, by a surprise movement or direction, through strong, dynamic movement. There might well be a minor climax in an earlier part as a result of a well-placed contrasting skill or a striking variation; but the major climax is the focal point of the composition.

To evaluate the water composition, apply the preceding principles objectively. Observe every aspect of the composition for its effectiveness. Does it give a feeling of delight and pleasure, or does it seem monotonous? Is there a sameness throughout that allows the attention to wander? Is there so much variety of patterns and techniques that there is a feeling of incoherence? Are any of the skills too difficult for the group to do? Do the skills and patterns build up to a high point? After some experimentation and changes, a satisfactory composition will be achieved.

SWIMMING—A GUIDE TO ACCOMPANIMENT

Creating a water composition that uses music as a stimulus and guide gives one an understanding of construction principles and a feeling for form. With the experience gained in choosing skills to synchronize with music and in developing them, with ingenuity, know-how, and ability to evaluate results, one has a background with which to create a water composition that does not rely upon music. As an aquatic creation takes shape independent of any musical support an accompaniment can be arranged to harmonize with it, and, now, the swimming is the guide to the form and character of the accompaniment. More than ever is it necessary to know musical terminology, rhythmic devices, and form in order to understand the construction problem of the accompaniment and thereby help to achieve unity between the swimming and the accompaniment.

Percussion and music especially written for the swimming are two means of accompaniment. Percussion is very suitable as an accompaniment for certain ideas. Of the many percussion instruments, the drum is probably the most satisfactory type because of the wide range of tonal quality which can be achieved through various kinds of beaters. An able and interested person could sound the underlying beat or rhythmic pattern on a drum and add tones from other percussive instruments or originate means for producing sound effects. Because of its melodic qualities, music has more emotional appeal and is more universally pleasing than the percussive instruments; one may be fortunate enough to have a dance accompanist or a gifted student interested in composing a musical accompaniment from which a record can be made.

COMPOSITIONS

"Successive Strokes," "The Aquacade," and "The Weaving Line" are examples of compositions which follow the principles just discussed. The skills used are basic ones and the music is of a simple structure.

SUCCESSIVE STROKES

THE THEME, THE PLAN, AND THE MUSIC. The idea of this simple composition is a succession of strokes, called a hybrid stroke (Plate 10), performed by two swimmers. The over-all plan of breaking the hybrid stroke down into its component parts and developing each part separately guides the designing of the choreography within the musical framework of the 112 measures of "Beautiful Ohio," a waltz, in Columbia album C-26.

THE WATER SKILLS. Synchronize the theme, four successive strokes, with a four measure phrase of the music—one measure for the arm pull of the breast stroke and the roll onto the side; one measure for stretching the arms apart on the glide of the side stroke and the roll onto the back; one measure for one arm pull of the back crawl and the roll onto the face; one measure for one arm pull of the front crawl. Be ready to repeat.

Other water skills used in the composition take two, four, or eight measures—two measures for one modified side stroke with the glide; two measures for one modified breast stroke with the glide; four measures for one somersault, fast dolphin, or one porpoise, coming up into position for the next skill; eight measures for one shark circle.

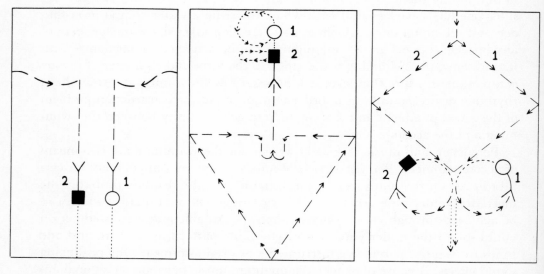

Fig. 44.   Fig. 45.   Fig. 46.

Successive Strokes

THE COMPOSITION

Figure	Starting Position	Measures
44	One swimmer dives in from each side of the pool and comes up in the center, facing down pool.	8

Execution

	Swim four thematic strokes down the center of the pool. Stand on bar 16 instead of making the last arm pull, in preparation for the modified breast stroke.	16
45	Swim six modified breast strokes—four to the wall, one while changing directions, and one toward the center of the pool.	12
	Take one porpoise dive, turn under water, and come up in back and front crawl tandem position but not attached.	4
	Swim four crawl strokes up the center of the pool—swimmer 1 doing back crawl and 2, front crawl.	8
	1 does a fast dolphin and 2, a porpoise dive. They come up in reverse position to repeat front and back crawl down the pool.	4
46	Swim two crawl strokes—swimmer 1 doing front crawl and 2, back crawl.	4
	Facing center, swim four modified side strokes with the glide diagonally to the side of the pool.	8
	Swim four modified side strokes diagonally to the center.	8
	Make one shark circle.	8
	Swim two back crawl strokes to the shallow end.	4
	Do one back somersault. Prepare for the restatement. Swim four thematic strokes up the center.	4 16
	Porpoise dive and swim under water, each to a ladder. Emerge onto the surface as the music ends.	8

                                                                    ———
                                                                    112

THE AQUACADE

THE THEME, THE MUSIC, AND THE PLAN. The theme, which is based on a water skill, is the front-crawl stroke synchronized by twelve swimmers. Play the waltz "Over the Waves" (Victor twelve-inch record, 35798) at a slow tempo.

Planning for a group of twelve swimmers in a 30- by 60-foot pool is quite different from planning for two. When the group moves the length of the pool, there is the problem of what to do with those who arrive at the opposite end first. However, this very problem is a guide to making interesting designs. This is illustrated at the end of the first part of "The Aquacade" when the group fans out from the two vertical lines to form a solid square, which provides a climax to that part. Floating patterns are most successful with a large number of swimmers, and for this reason the accordion is introduced and developed in the middle part of the composition. The restatement of the crawl stroke uses a short form of composition as a guide for designing.

THE WATER SKILLS. From the moment the swimmer leaves the side of the pool until he emerges onto the surface of the water, the standing dive takes four measures. The crawl stroke synchronizes with two measures and the reverse crawl turn introduced in the restatement should be performed without taking additional measures. The floating pattern of the circular accordion, which unfolds into a long line accordion, and the small revolving ones make a spectacular sequence. Change from one pattern to another according to the phrasing and sectioning of the music.

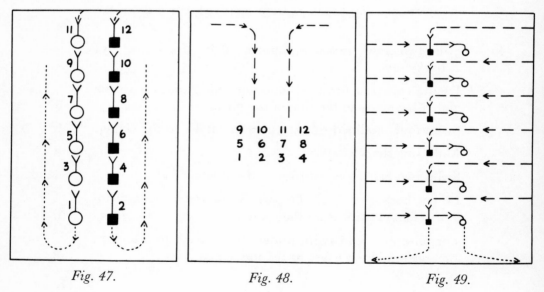

Fig. 47.   Fig. 48.   Fig. 49.

Aquacade

THE COMPOSITION

Figure	*Starting Position*	*Measures*
	Each of six pairs of swimmers walks to the edge of the pool at the deep end, one pair every four measures. Each pair stands in readiness to dive for four measures, then dives in succession, every four measures.	32

Execution

47   Each pair swims front crawl down the center of the pool. Partners turn away from each other at the shallow end and crawl back to the deep end.

48   Partners meet and swim close together down the center, fanning out into four rows of three in the center of the pool.   64

       All twelve swimmers form a double circle.   4

36   Form a circular accordion and revolve.   32

37   Open out into a long line accordion.   32

38   Break into three small accordions of four each and revolve. Rejoin into the line accordion. Release hold of adjacent person and back crawl splash kick back to the side walls.   32

       Crawl across, weaving horizontal lines.   8

49   Reverse turn and, after passing in center the second time, make right angle turns and front crawl to exits.   24

                                                        ———

                                                        228

THE WEAVING LINE

THE THEME, THE PLAN, AND THE MUSIC. The water pattern of a vertical weaving line of eight crawl swimmers is the theme and the over-all plan of breaking down the line and building it up guides the designing of the composition. The weaving idea persists in the development of the contrasting ma-

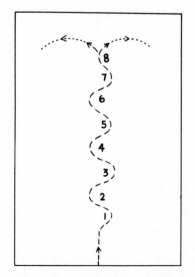

Fig. 50. The Weaving Line

terial in the middle part and in a short transitional pattern of diagonal weaving that follows. This diagonal crossing of two lines is the climax of the composition, as the restatement which follows is an exact repetition of the vertical weaving lines of the first part. Follow the *A B A* plan although no music accompanies the swimming. A suitable musical selection could be located and the water composition adapted to synchronize with it.

THE WATER SKILLS. A shallow dive, the crawl stroke, breast stroke, and porpoise dive are the skills used. The tempo of the swimming is the usual rate of two measures for one crawl stroke or one breast stroke and four measures for a porpoise.

THE COMPOSITION

Figure   *Starting Position*

Eight swimmers dive into the shallow end of the pool at successive intervals, starting with 1.

Execution

50   Swimmers front crawl up the center of the pool to their respective places, weaving in and out among those who preceded them and who are treading water. As 8 passes 1, 1 and the others in succession continue to follow through the weaving line.

The Weaving Line

51   The original pattern of eight swimmers divides into two like patterns of four each repeating the weaving line, and then into four lines of

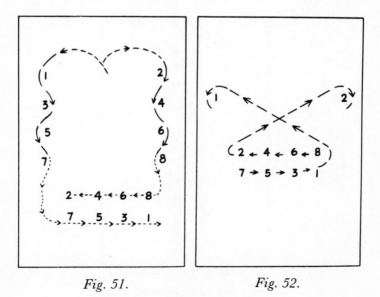

Fig. 51.   Fig. 52.

The Weaving Line

two. The end swimmer in each of the four vertical lines dives under the swimmer in front. The next four in back repeat the dive.

52   The four vertical lines of two, now treated as two horizontal lines of four, cross through each other diagonally and again form the two weaving lines of four, followed by the one weaving line of eight.

8

STAGING

To stage a program means to add a theatrical atmosphere to the demonstration by the use of choral music, lighting, sound effects, properties, costumes, setting, or acting. Water techniques lend themselves well to effective staging, which provides a spectacular means to display the swimming skills. Staging effects vary from the simple to the complex and may be combined with any type of swimming skill. Their use and complexity depends upon the ingenuity, money, and manpower available to produce them.

In the suggestions that follow, more than one theatrical aspect may be present in a number, such as both lighting and music. In some suggestions, acting ability is extremely important.

MUSICAL EFFECTS

Musical accompaniment can be of great value in synchronized swimming programs as a basic factor in defining the mood and theme of the composition. The following examples illustrate how the singing of a choral group can be effectively integrated with the swimming to produce a water composition with both dramatic and musical interest.

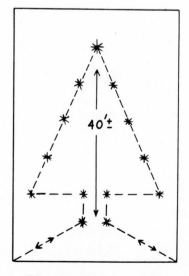

Fig. 53.   Christmas Tree

130

A Christmas Carol. A quartet sings "Adeste Fideles" or some other carol as thirteen swimmers with lighted candles walk down the steps of the pool and in unison swim on their sides into the outline of a big Christmas tree (Fig. 53). They tread water for a minute while the singing continues, then swim out of the pool, maintaining the outline of the tree. The singing ends as the last candle is carried out of the water and extinguished.

A Toast. A large number of swimmers, holding onto the edge of the pool with one hand and raising an imaginary cup with the other as if offering a toast, gurgle part of "Drink to Me Only with Thine Eyes."

A College Song. See page 131 for a description of "You Can Tell That I'm a Freshman."

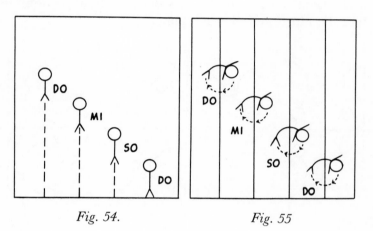

Fig. 54.   Fig. 55

String Quartet

The String Quartet. This act illustrates how accompaniment can be improvised. Do-Mi-So-Do, four notes of the scale, are each represented by a singer and a swimmer. The lane lines lengthwise of the pool simulate the strings of the instruments, hence the string quartet. The rhythm and tempo for the water skills used to swim over and under and up and down the strings are beat on a kickboard with a puck. The swimmers build the water skills into a composition and the four singers create the singing accompaniment with variations in tempo, volume, length of notes, repetition of notes, and chords following a design for short water compositions. This original act requires considerable practice on the part of both singers and swimmers.

A possible statement: Four swimmers stand outside the shallow end of the pool and as the four notes, Do-Mi-So-Do, are sung in succession, held as a chord, and repeated, the respective swimming "notes" dive in and synchronize their crawl strokes in a diagonal pattern up the pool (see Fig. 54).

A possible development: As the singing notes sing chords of two, three, and four notes, the swimming notes dolphin and porpoise dive in unison over and under the strings (Fig. 55).

The Campfire. A group sings campfire songs as sixteen swimmers synchronize floating and swimming patterns around a wooden support with a fire burning in the center. The support consists of two 2 x 4's, each 16 feet long, which are crossed at right angles and braced near the center. The central area holds a metal basin. The counselor lays the fire in the basin, pouring kerosene over the wood to insure an immediate flame. The wooden support may be floating behind the dock and moved into position when ready for use. Anchor it by means of a weighted chain.

Four of the swimmers, carrying lighted tapers, swim in and light the fire as the rest of the group front crawl stroke around the support—all to the choral accompaniment of "Each Campfire Lights Anew". The sixteen swimmers then synchronize their strokes and float to "Drifting and Dreaming," "The Call of the Fire," and "Father Time."

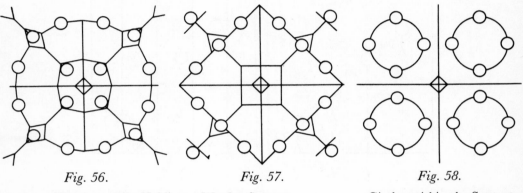

Fig. 56.   *Fig. 57.*   *Fig. 58.*

Floating while Holding a Wooden Support   *Circles within the Support*

The following suggestions make effective patterns for the composition:

The swimmers with head, arms, and legs showing, float. Those with only head and arms support the floaters by treading water and holding to the wooden support (Figs. 56 and 57).

The swimmers lie on their backs forming a joined circle around the wooden support. They scull with the outside arm (see Fig. 18).

Four swimmers in each section join hands and synchronize scissors kick, moving in a circle (Fig. 58 and Fig. 42c).

Synchronize front crawl stroke, following the outline of the wooden support. Make all angle turns simultaneously.

End the composition with splash kicking which extinguishes the fire and permits the removal of the wooden support in darkness.

OTHER SOUND EFFECTS

The swimmers themselves can make sound effects by splashing, swishing, and slapping the water to simulate the sounds and spray of the ocean, to emphasize the accents of the music, or to provide a background for advanced exhibitions.

SPLASHING. Although one of the main characteristics of synchronized swimming is smooth and quiet kicking, front and back crawl splash kicking can be used occasionally where an accent or special effect is desired. Splash kicking is executed by a forceful and exaggerated movement of the legs with the knees slightly bent. Vary the effect by gradually increasing the volume and cutting it off abruptly at the end or by swelling the volume (gradually increasing and then decreasing the amount).

Use the splash kick to simulate a fountain. The swimmers form a circle and synchronize their porpoise dives to the center, come up together holding hands, and scull backward and forward, increasing and decreasing the splash as the circle grows larger and smaller (see Fig. 34, a and b).

Splash kicking makes an interesting background for advanced skills. Two examples of an effective use of splashing for a background follow:

1. A large group of swimmers place themselves evenly along both sides of the pool, hold on, and break the water with the back crawl kick. During the splashing, duos and trios synchronize water skills up and down the center of the pool. The splash may remain the same volume until the end, or the volume may swell as the skills performed in the center vary in their degree of difficulty or effectiveness.
2. Two lines of swimmers on the sides of the pool weave horizontally or diagonally across the pool, using back or front crawl splash kicking. At the same time two or three swimmers in single file synchronize strokes up and down the pool following through the center opening made by the weaving lines.

Use the splash in the entrance or exit of a large group. For example, the group is evenly divided, placed opposite spaces, and are holding onto the sides with both hands, facing the pool and with feet up against the pool in a crouched position ready to spring. On signal they push hard up and out, throwing arms over their heads, and back crawl kick to the center forming one long line—the push off making splash as well as the kick. In this line all turn and synchronize the crawl stroke down the pool and exit; or start swimming a routine.

A variation for the beginning of a rountine is to push off to the center, as described, roll onto the face with arms in front, and crawl kick across the pool.

SWISHING. To swish, sweep an outstretched arm in a semi-circle across the surface of the water. Swishes can be loud or soft; for a soft swish, the arm should barely cut the water.

A storm and waves lapping the shore is easily effected by using splash kicking and arm swishing. In designing the sound pattern, listen carefully to the sounds created and consider their spacing. Create an impression of rough sea by a slow, steady rhythm and by increasing and decreasing the volume of two different arm and leg movements. Use twelve swimmers for the following routine, spacing six swimmers wide apart along the length of each side of the pool. Each holds on with both hands and lies on his back ready to kick.

All synchronize 15 loud back crawl splash kicks; 15 medium loud kicks; 15 soft kicks.

Drop legs and hold onto the gutter with the left hand. All synchronize 2 regular swishes, 1 soft swish; 3 regular swishes, 1 soft swish; 2 regular swishes, 1 soft swish. Repeat this order of swishes.

Hold onto the pool as in the beginning and all synchronize 15 soft splash kicks; 15 medium loud kicks; 15 loud kicks.

PERCUSSIVE SOUNDS. Percussive sounds may be made by the swimmers themselves by slapping the water in back while swimming (see page 40).

LIGHTING

Lighting equipment used in the room or manipulated by the swimmers, such as spotlights, underwater lights, luminous paint, candles, sparklers, and battery lights, provide many striking effects. The room should be in darkness. Remember that it takes time for a spectator's eye to adjust to the change from light to darkness and vice versa. When lighting becomes brighter, it takes only a few seconds for the adaptation, but when lights are turned out, it takes a minute or so for the eye to adjust. This fact is especially important to consider when using luminous paint.

POOL LIGHTING. Soft, diffused underwater light is excellent for demonstrating stunts and underwater swimming, singly and in groups. The silhouette of both the diver and the swimmer is accentuated because the light comes from below. The spectator sees the finish of a dive and the ascent of the diver from the bottom of the pool very clearly with this kind of lighting.

Four of these underwater lights are sufficient to illuminate two-thirds of a 60-foot pool, the deeper section. Waterproof underwater lights are attached to brackets or steel pipes which conduct the wire over the pool edge and through the water from a light socket. All joinings require waterproofing and a licensed electrician should make the installation and supervise the use of the lights. Any local laws involving the use of underwater lights should be observed.

A spotlight focuses attention on a particular act or person. The fact that it is maneuverable and encompasses a limited area should be considered in planning for its use. A wheel of gelatine colors used in front of a spotlight softens the brightness and produces a different atmosphere. The illusion of a rainbow may be created in this manner.

EQUIPMENT CARRIED BY THE SWIMMERS. Candles, sparklers, and luminous objects carried by the swimmers add to the effectiveness of a water composition. However, whenever swimmers carry equipment their arm action, of necessity, is limited.

A candle burns and a luminous object glows more or less indefinitely; the light from a sparkler is limited. A 20-inch sparkler burns for three minutes; a 36-inch sparkler burns for five minutes. Sparklers, in contrast to the steady glow of candles or luminous objects, give a flashy effect.

Examples of how swimmers can use sparklers, candles, and luminous objects in compositions follow:

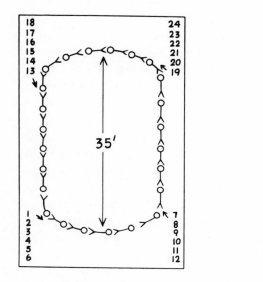

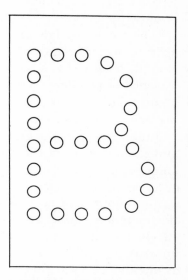

Fig. 59.   Oval   Fig. 60.   Forming a Letter

1. As a finale to a program, swimmers can form an initial of their school or club. For example, to form the letter *B*, use twenty-four swimmers. Six swimmers at each corner of a 60-foot pool carry three-minute sparklers. The first swimmer from each corner enters the water with a lighted sparkler. In turn, the other five follow the leader. All synchronize the side stroke and form a large oval (Fig. 59). This takes about one and a half minutes. At signal, all tread water. Those on the right side of the circle walk in to form the letter *B* while swimmers on the left side form a straight line (Fig. 60). This takes thirty seconds. At a signal, all return to the original formation and each goes out by the exit by which he entered. This takes one minute.

2. To dramatize a composition for a special occasion, such as Christmas, Easter, or a birthday celebration, see "A Christmas Carol," page 131.

3. For a mock graduation ceremony, diplomas (rolled sheets of paper with a two-inch band of luminous paint across the top) are awarded to a group of swimmers who enter the water one by one and synchronize the side stroke as they form the initial of their school. Hold this letter formation while a group outside the water gives one of the school's short cheers. See that all the swimmers hold the diplomas the same way so the letter will be even.

EQUIPMENT WORN BY THE SWIMMERS. Colored lights or luminous-painted articles worn by the swimmers produce striking effects and do not restrict the swimmers' choice of strokes as much as candles, sparklers, or luminous objects which must be carried.

Breast and overarm strokes are preferable when colored lights are used. If stunts are performed very far under water, the lighting effect may be blurred; hence such stunts should be avoided. Diving from the board is not effective because the outline of the diver's body does not show.

These colored lights are Christmas tree bulbs, spaced about ten inches apart on a rubber-covered wire. One set is strung up the swimmer's arms and extends from wrist to wrist; another is strung up both legs. Each string is attached to two dry cell batteries which are held at the back by a belt worn around the waist. The swimmer can turn on the strings by pushing either of the switches at his back.

Luminous paint* is easy to manage and is satisfactory where the settings and costumes are in the dark for only a short time. Articles painted with luminous paint may be used effectively more than once in the same program, or for several programs, if they are activated by light before every use.

Luminous-painted products glow in the dark after exposure to light, a phenomenon known as phosphorescence. The surroundings must be completely dark and the glow, although it continues for several hours, is strongest immediately after exposure. Ultra-violet products glow in the dark as long as ultra-violet light (blacklight) is turned on them, a phenomenon known as fluorescence. Regular spotlights of 500-1000 watts equipped with ultra-violet glass filters are necessary to produce the fluorescent effect. The latter method is recommended where the effect is required over a period of time. It is also brighter. In all cases it takes a minute or two for the eye to adapt to the darkness. Experiment before the performance with the luminous-painted articles to be certain that the painted area shows up well from the position of the spectators. Examples of the use of luminous objects follow:

1. The swimmers wear white gloves, caps, and socks. Paint the entire back of the gloves, including the fingers, and have the swimmers use the front crawl stroke. Paint the fore part of the socks over the instep to the toes if stunts and swimming on the back are performed. Paint strips of waterproof adhesive stuck on caps while stretched on a head. The area of the cap covered with adhesive and paint depends on the position of the spectators in relation to the pool. A large area should be visible. Expose the articles to light before using them and allow time for the eyes to adjust to the darkness.

2. Have a "skeleton" emerge from behind a curtain hung in back of the diving board. His costume consists of black tights with a life-sized skeleton cut from white muslin, covered with luminous paint, basted onto the tights both in front and back. Instead of the tights, he could wear a black leotard,

*Obtain information concerning luminous paint and ultra-violet lighting from Stroblite Company, 75 W. 45th St., New York, New York.

hockey stockings, and gloves all sewed together. Put the top of a black stocking with holes cut out for the eyes over his head and attach it at the neck of the tights to complete the covering.

SETTING, COSTUMES, AND PROPERTIES

All settings, costumes, and properties should be simple and easy to manage. Build the program on a central idea, using one setting for the entire performance. Use a backdrop, stage properties, and costumes that are suggestive of the idea rather than completely portraying it. In all cases, whether setting or costume, display the suggestion boldly. A swimming pool room is large and the audience is not too close to the scene of activity so that staging must be on a large scale in order to make the picture satisfactory.

WATER PROPERTIES. The following are suggestions for water properties:

1. Cards and similar objects dipped in melted paraffin to waterproof them.
2. Small lead weights to hold objects on the bottom of the pool. Two small weights fastened about 15 inches apart onto a large hoop will hold it down on the bottom of the pool in a vertical position, and porpoise dives and dolphins may be performed through the hoop.
3. Luminous paint on adhesive for markers on the pool edge or diving board end for swimming and diving in the dark.
4. Oil cloth, plastic cloth, waterproof adhesive, wire to shape flowers and other articles, gummed rubber tape, balloons, and corks.

EXAMPLES OF SETTINGS, COSTUMES, AND PROPERTIES. To show how effective simple settings and costumes can be, three descriptions follow:

1. *Alice in Waterland.* A conversation between Alice and the Cheshire Cat coordinates the story and is the means of announcing most of the water program. The setting for this conversation is a huge cat's head, 8 feet wide, cut from a roll of brown paper, with the features and outline of the head painted to resemble the one in the famous Tenniel drawings. Hang the grin against the wall at the deep end of the pool. This makes a telling backdrop throughout the performance. Alice, in her costume, including the pinafore and headband, moves about near the cat as she talks with him. The cat's grin and Alice are sufficiently suggestive of the story to make a more elaborate setting unnecessary.

Theatrically enhance this setting by using luminous paint to cover the cat's features and the outline of its head, to paint Alice's head-band, pinafore, and a pair of gloves. Turn out the lights when the show is ready to start. Shortly the attention of the observers is focused on the cat's grin. Alice enters and the conversation starts. After the swimmers perform various numbers, during which the lights may be on or off, the show ends with the lights out and the luminous grin glowing again.

2. *Swymphony.* The setting is an orchestra with a conductor. The orchestra may consist of many instruments, each drawn large and cut out of carton board, spaced evenly along the two side walls of the pool. Paint the important features of each instrument and its outline two inches wide with luminous

paint. When the show is ready to start, turn out the lights so that the instruments around the pool glow. The conductor, with his collar, vest, gloves, baton, and socks in luminous paint, enters, bows, and conducts Swymphony for about one minute to a record played on the phonograph on his cue. Then he announces the program, and starts leading the various selections of music which furnish the cues for the swimmers.

3. *The Wedding of Hydrogen II and Oxygen.* The setting is a large room in a country club (the swimming pool) where both the wedding and reception are held for Oxygen and Hydrogen II. Have the bride wear a transparent shower curtain for a veil and carry a water polo ball with wired oilcloth flowers attached to a cover over the ball as her bouquet, which may be tossed and volleyed later. The bridesmaids wear huge colored oilcloth flowers on their shoulder straps, and the ushers, large white oilcloth carnations on their straps. The minister wears a black leotard and the parents dress in bathing suits, one representing a modern version and the other an old-fashioned type.

AQUA-SKITS

Aqua-skits can be planned for a group of persons who have both swimming and acting ability, for those who act well but cannot swim well, or for those who swim well but cannot act. Always consider the available swimming and acting talents of the group before choosing the skit. Very often acting ability can be detected during the course of normal activities in the pool. Some one will show a talent for mimicry, for pantomime, for comedy. Capitalize on this talent to keep the program light and entertaining.

Ideas for aqua-skits are endless. Impersonations or parodies require ingenuity, but are entertaining and easily produced. Students can use the words of a song as a guide for a water impersonation, create a picture of a person or "character" known to the audience, take off a situation or an event, dramatize a mock ceremony, swim to a reading of a story, or use pantomime to convey an idea. The following are examples of how various ideas can be used.

1. To the tune "You Can Tell That I'm Irish," have four persons sing "You Can Tell by the Flip in My Talk That I'm a Freshman" as a swimmer progresses up the pool, acting the part of a freshman. Then follow with "you can tell" versions for sophomore, junior, and senior, each in turn characteristically pantomimed by different swimmers in the water. Representatives of the different classes can be further distinguished by different costumes.

2. "Mr. Milquetoast" is a well-known comic strip character. Create an amusing picture of him as follows. Wearing an old bathing suit, hat, shoes, goggles, and carrying a towel and life ring or water wings, a student impersonating Mr. Milquetoast ambles along the side of the pool where others are putting on a program of swimming acts. He is afraid for the swimmers and attempts to toss the life saver; he gains a little confidence, pantomimes a few strokes on the side, and almost dives into the water. Then he becomes timid

again. As the last swimmer leaves the water, Mr. Milquetoast dares to jump in and to swim about choppily but happily to the shallow end. Suddenly he realizes he is in the water, panic overtakes him, and he dashes for an exit.

3. A water version of a blues song such as "St. Louis Blues" makes an entertaining duet. Have a boy and girl impersonate a dancing couple. The music will inspire them to improvise. Strokes and stunts in Chapters 4 and 5 offer water techniques with which to experiment. Make certain that the swimmers selected can convey the syncopated rhythm.

4. Have two or three swimmers with a flare for comedy take off a beautifully synchronized swimming number which has just been presented. The take-off routine should be well planned and complete. Use a trudgen stroke to give a bouncing effect in contrast to the smooth synchronized swimming. Exaggerate the high lights of the synchronized number and maintain a serious expression.

5. The "Gay Nineties" period is a good source for sketch ideas. Four girls wearing old-fashioned bathing suits* pantomime an act along the side of the pool, daring to put their toes in the water and almost swooning as a result. "By the Sea," "She's More To Be Pitied Than Censured," or some timely song may be sung by them or by others. They might sing "The Man on the Flying Trapeze" while a diver in a man's old-fashioned bathing suit does comedy or stunt diving.

6. Simulate a sidewalk cafe. Place four tables with chairs at one end of the pool. Four singing waiters set the scene. As they sing "Sidewalks of New York" or "In the Good Old Summer Time," four couples stroll in and each couple is seated at a table. Two waiters take orders at two tables. Then the four waiters join together and sing "Tea for Two" as two couples dive in and swim a synchronized number to the music. The swimmers return to their tables, and the waiters take orders at the other two tables. As they join together to sing "Cocktails for Two," the other two couples do a water routine.

7. This skit starts with a mother and her small child strolling along the pool edge. The mother tries to keep the child from playing in the water. At the deep end the child falls into the pool and the mother cries, "My child! Who will save my child?" A life guard, wearing a sailor's hat or a full costume, struts out at the opposite end and calls confidently, "I will save your child."

Mother: "Who are *you?*"
Sailor: "I am Jack Tar."
Mother: "Who is Jack Tar?"
Sailor: "I am Jack Tar of the U. S. Navy."
Mother: "Oh, U. S. Navy! Save my child!"

The sailor flings off his costume, dives in, and swims to the rescue of the child. The skit ends on a blissful note, with mother and child safely reunited.

*The Ocean Pool Supply Company, New York, and the Jantzen Knitting Mills, Portland, Oregon, will supply old-fashioned bathing suits to be worn only outside the water.

The conversation in this skit is traditional but the action may be modified in any way that suits the words.

8. A mock wedding of Oxygen and Hydrogen II with their attendants, parents, and a minister makes an appealing scene in the water. See costume suggestions on page 137.

The processional: An usher escorts the parents of the groom to the diving board. Another usher escorts the mother of the bride to a conspicuous place. The four bridesmaids and four ushers enter at the shallow end and literally walk in the water to their respective places in the usual slow tempo to the "Bridal Chorus" from *Lohengrin* where they tread water during the ceremony. The minister, groom, and best man enter from the deep end and tread water. The maid of honor and the bride on her father's arm walk up the center of the pool to meet the groom (Fig. 61).

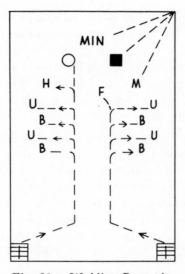

Fig. 61.   Wedding Procession

The ceremony: A parody of the ceremony, using chemical terminology, is spoken by the minister with the following lines as possible content—Minister: "Oxygen, wilt thou have this atom to be your lawfully wetted husband? Wilt thou swim by his side in high and low tide, love, honor, and keep him hydrated or dehydrated?" Oxygen: "I will" . . . Minister: Repeat after me. I, Hydrogen II, take thee, Oxygen, to be my wetted atom, to have and to hold, for better or for worse, through acid or alkaline, until electrolysis doth us part." . . . The best man drops the ring (a napkin ring) to the bottom of the pool.

The recessional: The bride, with the bouquet on the water between her arms, and the groom crawl down the pool to the exit to Mendelssohn's "Wedding March." The best man and the maid of honor, then the ushers and bridesmaids, synchronize their strokes and follow the bride and groom.

9. Have the following parody on a "Just So" story read, allowing time for pantomime.

"Once upon a time there were two little *tadpoles* who swished their tails around with great impunity. One day they found their arms and the impunity was doubled. What fun! Diving and leap *frogging* over one another.

(The evolution of the frog takes place in the center of the pool, building up to a climax in the shallow end. Tadpoles—two swimmers in prone position with arms at sides, heads out of water, crawl kick around a ten-foot circle in the deep end. As frogs, they do a choppy breast stroke side by side across the pool with faces out of the water, expressing glee; they swim one in back of the other across and scoop onto their backs for a choppy elementary backstroke. They surface dive down the pool, showing off to each other. In the shallow end they leap frog over one another croaking audibly as they exit.)

"But that was strenuous and they became so *weak* they *floundered* all over; and finally *perched* on a red lily pad.

(Pantomime in shallow water and use a red kick board for a lily pad.)

"As their strength came back, they started to sail. The wind was calm and the water was wet but they were the two most happy *sailfish* you ever saw, sailing right out to the deep ocean with that same impunity.

(Synchronize a series of sailfish (shark) stunts up the center of the pool to the deep end.)

"Out there they decided to *dolphin* and *porpoise* and porpoise and dolphin until I thought they would have been all upside down inside.

(Perform dolphins and porpoises in the deep end.)

"Maybe they were all upside down inside because they began to skim over the water back toward shore like beautiful *butterflies;* and I never saw them again."

(Synchronize butterfly strokes toward the shallow end and to exit.)

10. Build a skit around the idea of four horses, pulling an imaginary chariot in the water, commanded by a charioteer. Four swimmers, side by side and close together, synchronize "horse steps" around the pool. The charioteer remains constantly 7 or 8 feet in back of the "team," carrying a whip in one hand and calling commands.

The choice of steps may be guided by the personality of the team. The team may be a military one using an accented elbow lift and salute. The team may be spirited and impatient and "paw the ground" by making short quick pulls with the arm while in a vertical position; or by slapping a leg on the water while on the back. A forgetful "horse" may continue swimming when the others have stopped or may go in the opposite direction. A balky horse needs to be brought into line and reprimanded by the charioteer.

The charioteer may call each by name to which each responds by lifting or tossing the head or by "whinnying." He may call "Hep, two, three, four" several times to the military team at the end of their routine; the horses salute on *hep*. He calls all commands.

9

PLANNING A PROGRAM

A successful season logically culminates with a program that displays the accomplishments of the swimmers. The numerous water techniques, the many levels of swimming ability, the staging possibilities, competition, and the opportunities for creative work yield sufficient material to present satisfying, stimulating, and exciting programs. The type of program will be controlled by the aquatic ability and ingenuity available.

Fostering student leadership in planning and preparing a program is important. Through taking a constructive part in planning the program, student interest is created or increased. Under such conditions the swimmers perform to the best of their ability and with a spirit of enthusiasm and fun. Swimmers naturally vary in the value of the contributions they are able to make to program planning. The less experienced ones need practical ideas presented to them for consideration. The more experienced ones, on the other hand, have ideas of their own to offer, some of which are easily adaptable to the water and others, though they appear impractical at first glance, may be modified into a workable form. The teacher's added experience, wider contacts, and information enable her to contribute ideas and help as they are needed. This joint planning by teacher and students makes the production of a water program a cooperative venture which is one way to create interest and enthusiasm for an annual aquatic show.

THE BEGINNERS' PROGRAM

Everyone enjoys being a part of a swimming event. Plans must be carefully laid so that those in the beginning and intermediate classes can participate in a demonstration. So often preparation for these events must take place during regularly scheduled class hours, hence the following suggestions may be helpful for a simple production with inexperienced participants.

DATE. Schedule the demonstration for the end of the swimming season or term so that the ability of the various participants is known before definite plans are made. Sufficient time is thereby provided to develop and practice a routine of skills for each class or each level of swimming ability, built on skills learned in the classes. (See Chapter 3.)

PROGRAM AND PRACTICE. If rhythm has been emphasized in the process of teaching, if music has been used, or if swimming the skills in unison has been introduced, an excellent foundation upon which to build a program has already been laid. As each class, regardless of its level of ability, learns the skills, observe which skills are handled most easily. For smooth execution, the swimmers must perform the skills automatically. The quality of the execution, not the difficulty of the technique, impresses the onlooker.

From the skills that give promise of easy mastery at each level, choose those which allow most opportunity of diversity for the total program. Build a routine on each skill chosen. Gain variety by using different patterns for the routines, different skills at the various levels of ability, and music or other staging devices. Introduce competition in synchronized swimming between groups, even though the routines are simple.

If desired, one group may present more than one synchronized routine, or the better skilled ones in the class, two or more. There may be several classes of the same level of ability—for instance, three beginning groups. It is possible to teach the same routine to all beginners, especially if one teacher has all the classes, and for the swimmers to demonstrate it as a whole without practicing together. Unison is acquired and maintained by the use of the same rhythm and tempo in all three classes. There may be a class with more than one level of ability—such as beginners and low intermediates. In this case teach a routine to each group or teach the routine for the lower level to all.

Getting into position to start the routine offers an opportunity for the participants to dive or jump into the water at the deep or shallow end and swim to their places with a stroke different from the one they use in the routine. This informal start appeals particularly to beginners and low intermediates, many of whom have recently learned the skills.

Once the routine is established, have the class learn it and practice it each meeting thereafter. Some swimmers may need practice in addition to the class review. Because the skills are learned in the class periods, the practice serves a double purpose. Teach the other skills as the course progresses, but at some point in each class meeting review the demonstration routine. This constant practice increases the ease and precision with which the swimmers perform.

PERFORMANCE. Use a student leader of each group to check the members of his group as they arrive and handle any small problems that arise. The teacher or student may announce the order of events or a mimeographed program may be sufficient. The teacher conducts the routine.

THE ADVANCED PROGRAM

Time is essential for the planning, practice, and production of any program. The more elaborate the program is, the more time must be spent on its development. Skills and techniques must be at the swimmer's command.

THEME. Select a theme to use as a guide in the development of the program. Life, literature, and history present themes adaptable to water programs. Impersonations and parodies on events of local or current significance have great appeal. Abstractions or parodies on subject matter related to water —with ships, marine animals and characters, aquatic events, music and dance, theatre—are fitting themes. Select a catchy name for the program such as Pool Potpourri, Swymphony, Mermaid Miracles, Fishtail Fantasy (Frolic), Splashbacks, Aqua-tivities, Seaside Fashions, Water Ballet, Swimnastics, Rippling Rhythms.

Whatever the subject, the chosen theme guides the planning—the setting of the scene, the selection of the water activities, the appointment of the coordinator, and the writing of the lines. Costuming, setting, and speaking parts, though important, are not as important as the quality of the aquatics and their staging in an interesting and artistic way.

PROGRAM. Follow the general suggestions for either of two plans for the program. One plan stages chiefly synchronized swimming numbers, demonstrating only one type of activity. This kind of program may be monotonous unless care is exercised in planning. Gain variety by changing the number of swimmers in each act, through using various water techniques, by selecting several rhythms, and by introducing startling contrasts. Comedy numbers and aqua-skits which include swimming in unison are excellent.

The second plan includes many types of aquatic activities such as games, races, relays, life saving, and diving, with several synchronized swimming numbers as the high spots. By virtue of its variety, this plan provides many ways to interpret and develop the theme. It offers opportunity for all swimmers to participate—those who like to swim in unison as well as those who prefer to dive and race. Include from eight to twelve water activities in the program. Vary it by building up interest from the simple to the spectacular. A finale which includes all participants is effective. These suggestions offer variety for planning the water activities:

1. Synchronized swimming routines demonstrating skills learned in the classes
2. Synchronized swimming including stunts and floating patterns—for large groups, small groups, duos, and solos
3. Diving exhibitions
4. Life saving demonstrations
5. Competition—synchronized swimming events, official races and relays, novelty races, relays, and games
6. Aqua-skits
7. Entrance and finale

When competition is introduced, no fundamental change in the planning is necessary; but make provisions for judges, starter, and scorers. Races and relays are judged on the basis of speed; games, on the basis of points scored; stroke swimming, stunts, and diving, on the basis of form for which points are awarded. With regard to synchronized swimming and synchronized stunts, determine first whether the groups are to interpret the same idea, use the same music, have the same number of swimmers, and use staging effects. Then the judging may be on the basis of execution only or on composition and execution, the final result being an average of the two. Or the judging may be according to the rules set by the Amateur Athletic Union. Good competitive synchronized swimming adds excitement, and staging effects make striking contributions.

Program possibilities widen as the number of available synchronized swimmers increases, as swimmers become more versatile in their performance of water techniques, and as students learn to design their own compositions. To help coordinate the events and dramatize parts of the program, have a printed program or a master of ceremonies (coordinator).

THE COORDINATOR. The various water activities may be coordinated by someone portraying a popular character of the theme who gives the cues to the swimmers and maintains the interest of the audience between numbers. The coordinator should be a good actor and can be costumed for the part; he need not enter the water nor be a good swimmer.

He may present the program by a number of means: crystal gazing; dreaming or reminiscing; relating a story; reading a poem or story; writing or reading a letter; performing magic; announcing a radio broadcast, a game, or a concert; barking at a fair; traveling or sight seeing; pantomiming an interested spectator; conducting a program such as graduation, a fashion show, a class, a rehearsal, a party, a council ring, or a festival; turning the pages of a book, the hands of a clock, the pages of a calendar, or the pages of a concert or theater program.

The coordinator's lines should be short and clever and should include cues for the swimmers. After giving the cues for each event, he remains quiet while the aquatic number has the spotlight. To make the program move quickly, each group should know its cue well, be in position outside the pool, and ready to start on signal. The coordinator immediately takes control again when the water act ends.

SAMPLE THEMES

The themes that follow present ideas to show how water techniques and activities carry out the central idea of the theme. Both competitive and noncompetitive examples are given.

THE FISH BOWL. A seer, costumed for the part, looks into a large fish bowl and foresees a school of fish performing a number of water activities. His lines are in limerick form with a touch of humor. As he peers into the bowl and recites, each group in turn gets ready to perform. The seer unifies the program with the groups performing a variety of activities according to their ability. Activity suggestions follow:

1. Entrance—work out a marching routine for an entry into the pool.
2. Frogs practicing a routine—use the elementary backstroke by the beginners or the breast stroke by the advanced class.

3. The flying fish performing stunts—use diving; flying porpoises; dolphins; butterfly breast stroke relays.

4. Star fish putting on an exhibition—work out an outstanding diving or swimming act.

5. Craw(l) fish demonstrating crawl races and relays.

6. Phosphorescent fish exhibiting—use luminous paint with a synchronized swimming routine.

7. Exit—use a synchronized routine, saluting every fourth stroke.

THE NAVY VISITS HAWAII. The Admiral, a solemn, pompous person, co-ordinates the theme together with a lighthearted, comical first mate. Some-one blows "Assembly" on a bugle, and the Admiral announces to the fleet (swimmers representing ships of the Navy) that orders from Washington indicate full speed ahead to Hawaiian waters for naval maneuvers. Activity suggestions for the theme follow:

1. The fleet parades. All participants enter the shallow end and swim up the pool: ships—swim tandems on backs, carrying a silhouette of the state for which the ship is named; cruisers—swimmers dog paddle as they cruise a meandering path; destroyers—duos and trios synchronize racing dives and fast crawl strokes; aircraft carrier—swimmers kick a floating raft, each carrying a toy airplane in his mouth; submarines—several do the submarine stunt with the periscope.

2. Hawaiian dancers welcome the Admiral and first mate. Two girls dance along the side of the pool. The first mate flirts with them as they dance.

3. Hawaiian dancers show their affection for the Admiral by diving for pennies (synchronized stunts) and giving them to him.

4. The Admiral calls for naval maneuvers and announces the competitive events between the red and blue ships: target practice—divers perform all kinds of dives through a rubber ring; speed test for destroyers—swimmers race, using front and back crawl; torpedo practice—participants swim a relay across the pool, each member of the relay team punctures a balloon before the next in line can start swimming.

5. The Admiral announces shore leave; sailors choose partners and dance. Participants swim in pairs, using the various types of tandem swimming. Follow with the aqua-skit "Who Will Save My Child" (page 139), with the first mate as Jack Tar, the rescuer.

6. The Admiral announces that the fleet must leave Hawaii and that the night before departure they will conduct searchlight formation for their Hawaiian friends. The pool is darkened. Sailors wearing strings of lights perform a synchronized swimming number. With lights still out, the first mate plays "Aloha" on his ukulele while the fleet sings the song. All swimmers leave the room gradually so that the singing fades away in the darkness. When the lights appear again, the Navy has steamed away.

AQUATIC SCHOOL. Begin this theme with the skit "Who Will Save My Child" (page 139). The mother, elated over Jack Tar's rescue of her child, asks him where he learned his swimming skills. He, with great pride (and many funny gestures), reminisces about his aquatic school days. Suggestions for water activities follow:

1. Swimming fundamentals. Six swimmers synchronize slowly and smoothly, in a circular pattern, floating, sinking, bobbing, treading, walking, gliding. End with simple stunts.
2. Lifesaving strokes. The swimmers employ lifesaving routines to show the development of the side stroke and backstroke for lifesaving techniques.
3. Lifesaving releases. Demonstrate the releases through a skit. A big swimmer grabs a small scared swimmer, who impersonates Jack Tar. Carefully work out a series of holds and releases which give the effect of wrestling in the water. Use pivot parry, front and back holds and releases. Eventually Jack Tar tows the victim (big swimmer) in with the hair carry.

THE WEDDING AND RECEPTION OF H₂O. Carry out the mock wedding, page 140. Then continue with a reception in the water. Work out dancing numbers, have the bride toss her bouquet, and, through a relay, dress Oxygen and Hydrogen II for their wedding trip.

SPLASHBACKS. Using the graduation setting—with seniors assembled to receive their diplomas—seniors review the events of the past four years that have meant so much to them in a series of "splashbacks." Innumerable ideas can be developed for this program. The class president might act as coordinator.

SWYMPHONETTE. The theme is that of an informal concert with the co-ordinator acting as conductor. A setting such as that described on page 137 is effective. The printed program follows the style of a concert with the names of the musical compositions and their composers. Activity suggestions follow:

1. "Jalousie"—a tango by two swimmers wearing luminous paint
2. "Gold and Silver Waltz"—floating patterns (water studies)
3. "Pavane" (Gould)—a duet by "stray notes" with a spotlight
4. "Anchors Aweigh"—a synchronized marching activity
5. "The Man on the Flying Trapeze"—comedy diving accompanied by the singing of a quartet
6. "Adeste Fideles"—see A Christmas Carol, page 131.

AQUATIC DANCERS. Use a dance concert for the theme. A printed program announces the numbers with the names of the musical compositions, their composers, and the choreographers of the aquatic dances. Suggestions for water activities follow:

1. The entrance of the dancers—improvise a routine using the slap every fourth stroke, progressing in a snake-like line down the pool (see page 40). Perform this routine to a drum beat.
2. The folk dancers—execute swimming patterns imitating square dance routines.
3. The ballet dancers—practice turns and leaps and bar exercises in the shallow end of the pool, and improvise a stroke of a ballet type to coordinate the techniques with ballet leg stunts into a composition.
4. The acrobatic dancers—use diving and stunt swimming.

NEPTUNE. Neptune, the Roman god of the sea, lived in a palace at the bottom of the sea and, by waving his trident, controlled the waters and brought springs from rocks. He was also the god of horses. The Isthmian Games, comparable to the ancient Olympic Games, were celebrated in his honor. Chariot racing, torch racing, hurdling, hoop rolling, and discus throwing were the athletic events of those days. In the later Isthmian Games, music was an added feature. Symbols of Neptune are the trident, the dolphin, and the horse. Use this story to set the scene and write the lines. With Neptune as coordinator, conduct a competitive program. Ideas for competition follow:

1. The Isthmian Games (competition between groups)
   a. Represent hurdling by an obstacle relay or race; torch racing by swimming with a lighted candle; discus throwing by tossing a life buoy; hoop racing by rolling a water polo ball or by diving through a hoop (weight the hoop so it stands vertically on the bottom of the pool). Judge these events on the basis of speed and points scored.
   b. Represent chariot teams by synchronized swimming groups (see page 141). Judge the groups on originality and execution.
   c. Present aqua-skits based on the legend of the god Neptune. Judge the skits on originality and execution.
   d. Have each group perform a synchronized swimming number to the same music. Use the same number of swimmers in each group. Judge on composition and execution.

2. A Horse Show in Neptune's Honor (competitive events)
   a. Represent the various gaits of the "sea horses" and the manner of riding by form swimming: sidesaddle riders do the side stroke; canter, front, and back crawl strokes; gallop, the butterfly stroke; trot, the double-quick stroke; and the three-gaited "horse," a hybrid stroke of one breast, one side, and one front crawl arm pull. Judge on the basis of form.
   b. Represent jumping by springboard diving, or by stunts where springing from the bottom is possible. Judge on the basis of form. For a steeplechase, have an obstacle race; for a chariot race, use synchronized swimming teams. Judge these on the basis of speed.

3. Animals of the Sea (competitive stunts). Groups representing sea horses, sea cows (walruses), sea dogs (dogfish), sea hogs (porpoises,) sea lions (seals), sea serpents, dolphins perform stunts. Judge on the basis of form.

For a non-competitive program using the theme of Neptune, try the ideas below.

1. Use a routine which effects the sounds of the sea (see page 133) with Neptune quieting the rough waters by waving his trident, either as an opening or closing number.

2. Mermaids perform a synchronized number to the waltz "Over the Waves." Wearing luminous-painted caps and gloves, "electric eels" swim in the dark.

3. To develop the idea of Neptune bringing springs from rocks, have the swimmers develop a composition using the fountain splash (page 133). For example, wearing luminous painted caps, gloves, and socks, swimmers form a circle and make a fountain splash. As they enlarge the circle, a swimmer, also costumed in luminous paint, slips into the water, swims under water, and springs up from the bottom into the center of the circle. The circle opens and he swims alone or with the group, ending up in the center of the circle again, and sinking to the bottom of the pool as the splash closes in on him.

4. Have animals of the sea demonstrate stunts (page 145).

A FOOTBALL GAME. The drama and color of a fall football game with its acrobatic song and cheer leaders, its mascots, bands playing and marching formations present ideas that may be adapted to water. The participants are on one of two teams, and the audience is asked to take sides. The setting consists of a large score board and clock, a radio announcer and his equipment, and banners to indicate the teams and the cheering section. The radio announcer coordinates the events. Participants and cheerleaders enter as at a real game.

1. Before the game—cheerleaders direct the singing and cheering. Several swimmers accompany this with acrobatic diving and stunts in the water. The entrance of the mascots provides an idea for aqua-skits.
2. The first half—use a water ball, take sides, play half of an organized water game.
3. Intermission—present a synchronized swimming number which carries out the idea of a marching band and marching formations.
4. The second half—resume the water game.
5. After the game—announce the scores, direct cheers. Then all participants jump into the water and "celebrate" (splash kicking, slapping, acrobatic stunts).

THE OLYMPIC GAMES. Flags of the United Nations decorate the pool or form a setting at one end for a fire, real or simulated, which, after being lighted, burns throughout the event. Before the official opening of the Games a "marathon runner" crawls up and down the pool steadily for several minutes. He emerges from the pool, is handed a lighted torch, and lopes up the pool to light the fire. The contestants enter and stand under the flag of the country for which they are competing.

An official of the United Nations, the coordinator, opens the Games. There follows a procession of all participants, carrying their flags, ending with a tableau in the water before the United Nations official who administers the athlete's oath. Competition in various events follows. Include diving and swimming competition as well as competition in track and field events (novelty races and relays). Skating in the form of synchronized swimming may be introduced. Conclude with presentation of awards.

SCHOOL TESTS AND DEMONSTRATIONS. With this as a theme, innumerable events can be worked out on a competitive or non-competitive basis. The teacher is the coordinator. The pupils, in two teams, may be either fish or landlubbers. A possible entrance—synchronized marching into the room (up and down the pool) until each reaches his place. Have one or two pupils bring the teacher an apple. Suggested events—novelty races and relays to effect tests in reading, spelling, arithmetic; two quartets singing the same song in turn while fish and landlubbers do synchronized swimming to effect music classes or glee club demonstrations; dramatics; aquabatics (diving and stunts) to effect class work in swimming and diving or stunts and tumbling. A possible finale—marching in unison to the school song or forming the school initial in the water.

PROGRAMS WITHOUT THEMES

Consider a program of synchronized swimming numbers without the unifying element of an over-all theme. Thought for variety and contrast in the selection of music and skills, expression, costuming, and lighting makes for a well-rounded and interesting program. It is important to have the numbers follow one another quickly to avoid a lapse of attention on the part of the audience. The swimmers should get into position "off stage" during the number preceding theirs and at its close take their places on the pool deck or in the water. This allows sufficient time for the change in musical accompaniment or, if music is taped for the entire program, for them to be ready when their music starts.

LONG PLAYING RECORD: A BALLET SUITE. Ballet music dramatically illustrates an idea; a ballet suite consists of an arrangement of excerpts from the music of a ballet. A suitable long playing record of a ballet suite played through in its entirety offers an interesting part to a program. A familiar example is Tchaikovsky's Nutcracker Suite. An arrangement as played and conducted by the Austrian Symphony Orchestra and Kurt Wöss, RLP-190-87, is a 12-inch record that takes twenty minutes to play. It contains an Overture, March, Sugar Plum Fairy Solo, Russian, Araby, Chinese, and Flute Dances, and the Waltz of the Flowers, each having a playing time of from one to six minutes, with five to ten seconds between parts. Two or three groups of swimmers perform all the numbers; they assemble in the water around the edge of the pool before the ballet starts and, as each of the above compositions is played, the group of swimmers in that number performs; at the end of each one they return to the pool edge to await their next number.

10

CONDUCTING A ONE-DAY CLINIC

The best way to learn about synchronized swimming and to keep informed of the latest developments is to attend a clinic. At these scheduled gatherings teachers and students investigate and discuss topics of common interest, swimmers practice and demonstrate techniques, coaches and judges exchange ideas about exhibitions and competitions, and choreographers examine ideas for water compositions and pageants. One-day clinics, on a local or national level, are the kind most frequently held. These meetings can be stimulating to both the inexperienced or experienced teacher or official, and much subject matter can be covered if they are well organized and if the program is carefully balanced to interest all levels of abilities.

One competent leader and two demonstrators (for stunts, solo, and duet purposes) can stage a one-day clinic, though several leaders taking the responsibility for specific sessions and four to six demonstrators would be able to conduct a broader program. In any case, the leader must have assistants for the actual running of the event. These instructors or assistants can be drafted ahead of time or be drawn from the local group. The leader's responsibilities before the actual day of the class include determining the date, place, and number of sessions for the meeting; selecting and inviting leaders and demonstrators for the sessions; and disseminating information about the gathering to colleges, schools, and clubs in the area, through such media as mailings, press releases, and spot announcements on radio and TV.

A one-day clinic usually is divided into morning and afternoon sessions, and the leader must arrange the session program well in advance. A sample of the kind of program which might be arranged follows. It can readily be seen that the leader needs on-the-spot assistants for the day of the clinic to assure that registration and the sessions run smoothly.

	9:00-9:30	Registration
SESSION I	9:30-10:30	Introductory message
		Exhibition of a finished routine—solo
		Demonstration and explanation of basic stunts, simple stunts
SESSION II	10:30-11:30	Instruction and help to students on basic stunts
	12:00-1:30	Lunch
SESSION III	1:30-2:30	Discussion of choreography, music theme, composition, and costuming

151

Session IV	2:30-3:15	Demonstration and explanation of advanced stunts
Session V	3:15-4:00	Instructions and help to students on advanced stunts.
Session VI	4:00-4:30	Demonstrations of transitions from stunt-to-stroke-to-stunt
		Demonstration of a finished routine—duet
Session VII	4:30-5:00	Judging
Session VIII	5:00-5:30	Discussion on rules for competition

A few notes follow to give the clinic leader an over-all idea of procedures for the several scheduled parts of the one-day clinic.

Registration

Secure a desk and file cards.

Have each visitor enter his name, address, school or club affiliation, and indicate his position—instructor or student. These cards can be used later to mail clinic reports, if any, to participants or as a future mailing list.

Collect the fee, if any, for the clinic. This fee is undoubtedly necessary to help defray expenses incurred by the clinic.

Session I

Introductory message. Speak briefly on the values of synchronized swimming. Explain the purpose of the clinic. Suggest to the spectators certain aspects they should observe in the routine which is to be presented. These aspects include pattern in the pool, transitions, flowing movement, and synchronization with the music.

Exhibition of a finished routine—solo. Have the demonstrator present the routine.

Demonstration and explanation of basic stunts, simple stunts. Station the two demonstrators on the center line of the pool, facing opposite directions.

Have the first swimmer demonstrate a given stunt.

Then have the second demonstrator execute the same stunt. (With this system, spectators can better observe the stunt.)

Discuss the stunt. Offer teaching hints, mention common errors and methods of correcting them. Encourage questions from the audience.

Follow the stunt demonstration with:

1. Bobbing—emphasize its value in developing breath control.
2. Synchronized swimming strokes—point out the difference between these and standard strokes.
3. Sculling—emphasize how important sculling becomes as weight above the surface of the water is increased by the various ballet leg positions. Have the demonstrator scull on the back, head first; then with one knee drawn toward the chest; then in extended ballet leg position; and finally in double ballet leg position.
4. Basic groups of stunts—somersaults, dolphin, dolphin foot first, ballet legs.
5. Simple stunts—show a few progressions and combinations of these:

Porpoise	Dolphin, Bent Knee	Kip
Porpoise, Flying	Dolphin, Flying	Oyster
Somer-Sub	Dolphin, Chain	Tub
Walkover, Front	Walkover, Back	Submarine

SESSION II

Instructions and help to students on basic stunts. Secure instructors or assistants to work with the students in the pool. Divide the swimmers into as many groups as there are instructors.

1. Scull on back, head first.
2. Scull on back, head first with one knee bent.
3. Scull head first in single ballet leg position.
4. Execute somersaults, forward and backward, tuck and pike; dolphins. (Move from group to group, offering suggestions to instructors and to swimmers when necessary.)

SESSION III

Discussion of choreography, music theme, composition, and costuming. Have experienced teachers primed for this session. Show samples of costumes and head dresses.

SESSION IV

Demonstration and explanation of advanced stunts. Have all or some of the following executed by demonstrators. Explain execution procedures carefully.

Dolphin, Foot First

Dolphin, Foot First, Ballet Leg

Dolphin, Foot First, Submarine

Dolphin, Foot First, Bent Knee, One-half Twist

Dolphin, Foot First, Chain

Heron

Heron, Spinning

Swordfish

Catalina

Ballet Legs, Double

Submarine, Double Ballet Legs

Flamingo, Bent Knee

Flamingo

Barracuda

Barracuda, Spinning

Barracuda, Back Pike Somersault

Crane

SESSION V

Instructions and help to students on advanced stunts.

Following the demonstration and explanation of the advanced stunts, divide the swimmers into groups according to achievement levels and invite them into the pool for instruction and help. Use the same assistants who worked with the groups on basic stunts. Have them try the following:

Dolphin, Foot First

Dolphin, Foot First, Ballet Leg

Swordfish

Catalina

Barracuda, Back Pike Somersault

Following the last stunt, suggest that the students choose stunts with which they need help.

SESSION VI

Demonstration of transitions from stunt-to-stroke-to-stunt. Have demonstrators show several examples of smooth transitions.

Demonstration of a finished routine—duet. After calling attention to points discussed in previous sessions, have demonstrators present a finished routine. Encourage comments and questions after the presentation.

Session VII

Judging. Discuss factors involved in judging execution of stunts. Have demonstrator execute a Kip. Have members of clinic award grades on the Kip. Discuss these grades. Have a student execute a Kip. Have members of clinic award grades on the Kip. Discuss these grades.

Session VIII

Discussion on rules for competition.

11

COMPETITION IN
SYNCHRONIZED SWIMMING

Competition in any activity tends to produce a finer quality of performance. Under proper conditions, it may aid in the development of the individual in body, mind, and spirit. The proficiency required for competition demands a longer and more intensive training period, but the technical approach in training for competition is the same as that used in class instruction.

Simple competitions in the execution of stunts may be carried on during the class period to promote interest in synchronized swimming. As a student executes the stunt, the others in the group grade the stunt. It is important to follow this with a discussion on the reason for each grade awarded. In this manner the student becomes aware of the various factors which contribute toward good performance.

As the group progresses, simple routines may be presented and judged on choreography, interpretation of the music, synchronization with the music, or synchronization one with another. Later, individuals from other fields, such as music and art, may be invited to the class to offer suggestions and enter into the discussions.

Championship competitions are held in solo, duet, and team events from local to national levels in the United States and in several foreign countries. (The *Swimming Handbook* of the Amateur Athletic Union of the United States has detailed information on the conduct of an official synchronized swimming meet.)

STUNTS

In the area of synchronized swimming, various types of competition are employed. The least complex, and one of the most objective to judge, is a competition using stunts only. A list of required stunts may be used, or the list may include three required stunts and three optional stunts. A list of synchronized swimming stunts by groups appears on pages 161-162. Each required stunt should be selected from a different stunt group—for example, a dolphin, a ballet leg, and a kip would meet this requirement. The optional stunts should also be selected from different groups. The degrees of difficulty

155

should be taken into consideration, thus recognizing the ability of those who are able to execute the more difficult stunts.

The competition may be conducted as an intramural event or as a meet between high schools, colleges, or clubs.

OFFICIALS AND DUTIES. Personnel required to conduct this type of competition consists of at least three competent judges of execution of stunts, two secretaries, a referee, and two clerks.

Referee announces the stunt to be executed and signifies the moment at which the judges shall simultaneously flash the awards. The person selected should be one who has had experience with meets. In case of a controversy during a competition, his word is final.

Clerks see that the competitors are ready and that the swimmers execute the stunts in the proper order with no loss of time.

Judges seated in various positions around the pool, flash their awards simultaneously after each stunt is executed.

Secretaries record the awards, compute the score for the execution of each stunt, and determine the final score for each competitor.

METHODS OF MARKING. The use of a simple rating scale similar to that used in diving is recommended.

Completely failed	0
Unsatisfactory	½ – 2½
Deficient	3 – 4½
Satisfactory	5 – 6½
Good	7 – 8½
Very good	9　10

The awards of the three judges for the execution of each stunt are added and then multiplied by the degree of difficulty listed for that stunt in the Table of Difficulty Multiples for Stunts (see pages 161-162). The scores awarded each competitor on the required and optional stunts are added. The competitor receiving the highest score is the winner. In case of a tie the competitor receiving the highest score on the optional stunts is announced the winner.

MEET PROCEDURES. A written list of the optional stunts of each competitor must be submitted to the referee before the meet starts.

The competitors, having previously drawn for places, are divided into groups of six each. The first group of six lines up along the side of the pool where the stunts are to be performed. One clerk sees that the number one competitor is ready to execute the first required stunt. The referee announces the stunt to be performed and signals the competitor to start. After the stunt is executed, the referee blows the whistle, and the judges flash the awards simultaneously. The secretaries record and add the awards given by the judges, then multiply by the difficulty multiple, while the number one competitor is executing her second required stunt. The event continues in this manner until the first competitor has performed her three required stunts. Then the same procedure is followed by the five remaining girls in the group.

After group number one has performed the three required stunts, that group rests and group number two proceeds in the same manner for the judging of the required stunts.

After all groups have finished executing the required stunts, group number one returns to the water. Number one competitor performs her first optional stunt. Awards are flashed. Then her second and third optional stunts are performed and receive awards. Each member in each group follows the same procedure. With efficient organization, twenty swimmers may be judged in one hour.

Grade cards for judges may be made. The cards should be six by eight inches in size so that they may be read easily at a distance when shown by the judges. The cards must include all possible grades.

STUNTS AND A ROUTINE

A more complex competition consisting of two parts may be held. The first part consists of the execution of stunts as described above; the second part consists of the presentation of a routine. A requirement for the routine should be that it include a minimum number, perhaps four or five, standard stunts. The competitor must follow the routine submitted to the referee prior to the meet (see sample routine, page 163).

The judging of the routine is based upon:

1. The quality of the choreography—the construction of the routine and the interpretation of the music and the theme, by utilization of a variety of stunts, strokes and figures arranged to produce a unit of beauty and harmony.
2. Synchronization—the timing of stunts and strokes to the music and to the other members in the group (except in the case of solos).
3. Spectator appeal—the manner of presentation, including originality and showmanship.
4. Execution of the stunts and strokes within the rountine.

After the swimmer completes the presentation of a routine, the referee signals for the judges to flash their awards (one to ten) for the routine, first for the grade in Execution and then for Style which includes items 1, 2, and 3 above. The judges' awards are totaled to obtain the score for the routine.

In this type of competition, the final score is obtained by adding one tenth of the score awarded the separate competition in stunts, to the score awarded the routine.

The competition in the execution of stunts may be held in the morning, and the competition in the routines may be held in the afternoon or evening.

Three, five, or seven judges may be used. If either five or seven are used, the high and low awards may be eliminated, or all awards may be counted. The elimination of high and low awards is an especially good procedure if the judges have had little experience in judging.

ROUTINES WHICH INCLUDE COMPULSORY STUNTS

In this complex type of competition, a compulsory number of stunts, five for example, each from a different stunt group (see pages 161-162) must be included in the routine. The five stunts must be designated on a routine sheet (see page 164). The execution of the stunts and strokes is graded as the routine is presented in competition. At the same time the choreography, interpretation of the music, the synchronization, and the spectator appeal also have to be judged. It is most difficult to secure judges who have the ability to judge so many facets so quickly with any degree of accuracy.

In this type of competition two grades may be flashed, one for Execution, and one for Style, which includes all other factors involved.

The method of computing the score is as follows: For the Execution score, add the judges' awards and multiply by the average degree of difficulty of the five designated stunts—sum of the five difficulty multiples (see pages 161-162) divided by five; for the Style score, add the judges' awards. The final score is the sum of the Execution score and the Style score.

If one wishes to place still more emphasis on Execution than on Style, he may multiply the Execution score by a constant, before adding the Style score. A suggested figure for the constant is 1.3.

PLANNING A MEET
(Area Championship)

The synchronized swimming teacher or anyone who desires to conduct a competition should have a committee of three or four members to assist in planning the meet. The following general procedures may be modified to fit the needs of any particular competition.

Choose the committee from competent individuals among members of the school faculty, the Red Cross Water Safety Directors group, the city recreation staff, or the managerial staff of local pools. It is advisable for the synchronized swimming teacher to act as the meet manager. The committee makes decisions on the following items.

DATE. Set the date toward the end of the teaching season so that the competitors have the opportunity to put into practice some of the skills and knowledge they have been studying.

PUBLICITY. Mail information sheets to all interested schools and clubs in the area. Give releases to the press, radio, and TV stations. The information should include the date of the meet, the location of the meet, deadline for entries, rules governing the meet, events to be held, and name and address of the meet manager.

POOL. A satisfactory pool is one at least sixty by twenty-five feet, with water no less than eight feet deep in half of its area to permit the execution of stunts which require deep water. The water should be clear, the bottom of the pool white, and the light above the pool sufficient so that visibility is adequate for contestants, judges, and spectators. Room on the deck for entrances is desirable. An electrical outlet for the purpose of connecting a record player with loud-speaker attachment and microphone is necessary.

Locker and lounge facilities for competitors should be arranged. Have the pool available to competitors several days before the meet so that they may become familiar with entrance areas, exit ladders, and deep and shallow portions of the pool.

FORMS. The meet manager provides entry blanks for all contestants. They should be prepared, mimeographed, and distributed about four weeks prior to the date of the meet.

The entry form includes spaces for name, address of contestant, the school or club, the events included in the meet, date of the meet, time of each event, and the date by which all completed forms must be returned to the meet manager. This date should be at least three days prior to the competition.

DRAWING FOR ORDER. There should be a draw for order of appearance in the meet to insure an even chance for all contestants. (Many competitors consider the number one position undesirable.) At least an hour before competition starts, draw for places by lot under the supervision of the meet manager in the presence of officials, with a representative of each competing group, present. One method of conducting the drawing is to put the names of all contestants in a container and place the first name drawn in the number one position, place each successive name drawn in consecutive order. The meet manager records the order of appearance in the meet and gives copies to the referee, secretary, and announcer.

RULES. The rules governing the meet should be standard. The United States Amateur Athletic Union rules or those of the Division for Girls and Women's Sports of the American Association for Health, Physical Education, and Recreation are excellent.

JUDGING

Competent judges for synchronized swimming competition are very important to the swimmer and to the success of the meet. A good judge must have excellent qualifications in two areas: he must know the subject matter and he must be honest.

He must know the correct techniques involved in the execution of all the stunts. He should keep in mind a picture of perfect execution and check against it on points such as full extension, tight tucks and pikes, vertical and horizontal lines, height of the body in the water, slurred stunts, excessive arch of the back, the circles of dophin type stunts, and on flowing movement throughout.

He must be conversant with the elements which constitute a good choreography, which is the pattern through the water, balance of stunts and strokes, variety, originality, theme, and a fitting interpretation of the music. He needs some appreciation and knowledge of the construction of a musical composition. He needs to be aware of showmanship.

He must have the ability to make quick decisions and the courage of his convictions to stay with the decision. He should be able to justify his award. A catchy, novelty number should not confuse him nor should he be swayed by his personal opinion of the music or the theme at any time. He must be unhampered by bias and never be influenced by the opinions of others.

He should not be afraid to use both upper and lower sections of the grading scale. It is important that he differentiate between the good and the bad. True grading by comparison with perfection should always be used, regardless of the size or quality of the meet.

It is of help to some judges to keep in mind that *satisfactory* is a grade of 5. If the performer is better than satisfactory, add to 5; if he is not satisfactory, drop to a lower grade.

A person desiring to become a judge should attend clinics on judging, watch demonstrations of synchronized swimming in which the correction of errors is emphasized, confer with coaches and officials, make use of movies, slides, and books as training aids, and study the rules carefully.

LIST OF SYNCHRONIZED SWIMMING STUNTS BY GROUPS
and
TABLE OF DIFFICULTY MULTIPLES FOR STUNTS

I
Ballet Leg Group

	Difficulty
Ballet Leg, Single	1.5
Ballet Legs, Alternate	1.6
Ballet Legs, Double	1.8
Catalina	1.8
Catalina, Half Twist	1.9
Catalina, Full Twist	2.0
Catalina, Reverse	1.7
Eiffel Tower	1.6
Flamingo	1.9
Flamingo, Half Twist	2.0
Flamingo, Full Twist	2.1
Flamingo, Bent Knee	1.7
Flamingo, Bent Knee, Half Twist	1.8
Flamingo, Bent Knee, Full Twist	1.9
Submarine	1.5
Submarine, Double Ballet Legs	1.9

III
Dolphin, Foot First Group

	Difficulty
Dolphin, Foot First	1.7
Dolphin, Foot First, One-half Twist	1.8
Dolphin, Foot First, Full Twist	1.9
Dolphin, Foot First, Bent Knee	1.7
Dolphin, Foot First, Bent Knee, One-half Twist	1.8
Dolphin, Foot First, Bent Knee, Full Twist	1.9
Dolphin, Foot First, Ballet Leg	1.8
Dolphin, Foot First, Submarine	1.9
Dolphin, Foot First, Chain	1.8
Dolphin, Foot First, Pin Wheel	2.0
Figure Eight Dolphin, Foot First	1.9
Figure Eight Dolphin, Foot First, Variant	1.9

II
Dolphin, Head First Group

	Difficulty
Dolphin	1.5
Dolphin, Half Twist	1.6
Dolphin, Full Twist	1.7
Dolphin, Ballet Leg	1.6
Dolphin, Bent Knee	1.5
Dolphin, Bent Knee, Half Twist	1.6
Dolphin, Bent Knee, Full Twist	1.7
Dolphin, Flying	1.3
Dolphin, Flying, Half Twist	1.4
Dolphin, Flying, Full Twist	1.5
Dolphin, Flying, Double	1.5
Dolphin, Chain	1.6
Dolphin, Chain, Mixed	1.6
Dolphin, Pin Wheel	1.8
Figure Eight Dolphin	1.7

IV
Somersault Group
Forward and Back

	Difficulty
Barracuda	1.8
Barracuda, Spinning	1.9
Barracuda, Back Pike Somersault	1.9
Barracuda, Back Pike Somersault, Spinning	2.0
Heron	1.8
Heron, Spinning	1.9
Kip	1.6
Kip, Split	1.6
Kip, One-half Twist	1.7
Kip, Split, One-half Twist	1.7
Kip, Full Twist	1.8
Kip, Split, Full Twist	1.8
Porpoise	1.4

Porpoise, One-half Twist....... 1.5
Porpoise, Full Twist........... 1.6
Porpoise, Flying.............. 1.3
Porpoise, Flying, Double....... 1.5
Propeller.................... 1.2
Seal........................ 1.5
Somersault, Back Pike......... 1.4
Somersault, Back Tuck......... 1.1
Somersault, Forward Pike...... 1.2
Somersault, Forward Tuck..... 1.1
Somersault, Tandem........... 1.2
Somer-sub 1.5

V

Diverse Group

Difficulty

Corkscrew.................. 1.2
Crane...................... 2.0

Log Roll.................... 1.1
Marching on Water........... 1.1
Marlin..................... 1.2
Monkey Roll................ 1.3
Muskrat.................... 1.3
Oyster..................... 1.2
Pendulum................... 1.7
Pendulum with Reverse....... 1.9
Plank...................... 1.4
Shadow Stunting
   (stunt difficulty +)......... .1
Shark...................... 1.2
Shark Circle................ 1.3
Shark Figure Eight........... 1.5
Spiral..................... 1.8
Swordfish.................. 1.7
Tailspin.................... 1.9
Torpedo.................... 1.3
Tub....................... 1.1
Walkover, Back............. 1.4
Walkover, Front............. 1.4
Water Wheel............... 1.3

ROUTINE SHEET

Solo	Duet X	Team

Check Proper Square

Name   Title of Meet

Representing

Theme   Address of Meet

Music   Day Month Year

ROUTINE

Entrance (Land Movements—Slide in)
Back Crawl   (Modified)   3
Dolphin, Foot First, Figure Eight
Kip
Side Stroke   (Modified)   4
Ballet Leg, Single
Flamingo, Full Twist
Hybrid Strokes   (Back, Side, Crawl)   3
Somer-sub
Hybrid Strokes   (Back, Side, Crawl)   3
Heron, Spinning
Shark Circle
Hybrid Strokes   (Breast, Side, Crawl)   4
Porpoise
Dolphin, Foot First, Bent Knee, Full Twist
Scull Downward, Swirl and Drop below Surface of Water to Exit

AWARD

JUDGE

JUDGE'S GRADING SHEET FOR
SYNCHRONIZED SWIMMING ROUTINES

Solo	Duet	Team
	X	

MARK X ACROSS PROPER SQUARE

Sally Smith
Mary Jones
_____
NAME

Women's Indoor
National Synchronized
Swimming Championships
_____
TITLE OF MEET

Order of Draw 3

KRNT RADIO and TV
Des Moines, Iowa
_____
REPRESENTING

Illinois Athletic Club
Chicago
_____
ADDRESS OF MEET

Place of Finish 2

Nassau Motif
_____
THEME

_____
MUSIC DAY MONTH YEAR

STUNT GROUP NUMBER	NAME OF STUNT	MARK COMP. STUNTS WITH X	DIFF.	DIVIDE SUM OF DIFFICULTY MULTIPLES 8.5 by 5 TO ARRIVE AT AVERAGE DEGREE OF DIFFICULTY FOR ROUTINE 1.7
	Entrance (Deck Movements—Slide in)			
	Torpedo			
3	Figure Eight Dolphin, Foot First	X	1.9	
	Side Strokes (Modified)			
	Ballet Legs, Alternate			
4	Kip	X	1.6	
	Hybrid Strokes			
2	Dolphin, Ballet Leg	X	1.6	
	Hybrid Strokes			
5	Walkover, Back	X	1.5	
	Hybrid Strokes			
	Porpoise			
1	Flamingo, Half Twist	X	1.9	
	Exit in Water			

JUDGE NO.	1	2	3	4	5	Total	X Ave. Diff	
AWARDS FOR EXECUTION	7	7½	8	8	7½	23	1.7	39.1
AWARDS FOR STYLE	7½	8	8	8	8	24		24

P. Stephens
JUDGE

Cullen
SECRETARY

Holan P.
REFEREE

TOTAL SCORE 63.1

DATE DUE

GAYLORD			PRINTED IN U.S.A.